NATIONS of the WORLD

SAMUEL BRIMSON

Library of Congress Cataloging-in-Publication Data available
upon request from publisher. Fax (414) 336-0157 for the attention
of the Publishing Records Department.

ISBN 0-8368-5491-8

This North American edition first published in 2004 by
World Almanac® Library,
330 West Olive Street, Suite 100, Milwaukee, WI 53212 USA.

Created by Trocadero Publishing, an Electra Media Group
Enterprise, Suite 204, 74 Pitt Street, Sydney NSW 2000, Australia.

Original copyright © 2003 S. and L. Brodie.

WORLD ALMANAC® LIBRARY

Sierra Leone

REPUBLIC OF SIERRA LEONE

Sierra Leone is on the Atlantic coast of western Africa. The interior is grassland or forest, while the coastal plain is dominated by swamps. There are small mountain ranges in the east. The climate is tropical with a wet season from April to November.

The population of Sierra Leone is made up of about 20 ethnic groups. The largest are the Mende in the south and the Temne in the north. More than half the people follow Islam, while some thirty percent practice animist religions. About ten percent are Christians. English is the official language.

The original Bulom inhabitants were joined by the Krim and Gola peoples in the fourteenth century A.D. A century later the Mende arrived. The country was named Sierra Leone, meaning lion mountains, by the explorer Pedro de Cintra, who visited the coast in 1460. Portuguese traders settled shortly thereafter. They dealt in timber and ivory. The sale of slaves was especially lucrative. The British Antislavery Society established a colony at Freetown in 1787 for former slaves from the U.S. and Britain.

Great Britain made Freeport a crown colony in 1808. It became a protectorate in 1896. Free elections for a legislative council began under the 1924 constitution. Sir Milton Margai became chief minister in 1954.

Sierra Leone became an independent nation on April 27, 1961, with Margai as prime minister. Siaka Stevens was elected prime minister in 1967. He was removed from office for a brief time, due to a military coup. Guinean troops aided in preventing a coup in 1971.

Sierra Leone became a republic in 1971, with Stevens as president. He created a one-party state in 1978. Elected in 1986, Joseph Saidu Momoh revived multi-party democracy five years later. Captain Valentine Strasser deposed Momoh in 1992. He was removed four years later. Civilian Ahmad Tejan Kabbah was elected president in 1996.

The Revolutionary United Front (RUF), made up of local dissidents and Liberian guerrillas, fought an increasingly bloody battle with government troops beginning in 1991. Kabbah was ousted from office in 1997. The first group of 6,000 United Nations peacekeepers arrived in 1999. The following May, 500 of those people were kidnapped by RUF members. British forces and 10,000 more U.N. troops finally brought the situation under control. A cease-fire agreement was signed in late 2000. The much-postponed May 2002 elections returned Kabbah to office.

GOVERNMENT
Capital Freetown
Type of government Republic
Independence from Britain
April 27, 1961
Voting Universal adult suffrage
Head of state President
Head of government President
Constitution 1991
Legislature
Unicameral Parliament
Judiciary High Court
Member of CN, IMF, OAU, UN, UNESCO, WHO, WTO

LAND AND PEOPLE
Land area 27,600 sq mi
(71,740 sq km)
Highest point Loma Mansa
6,391 ft (1,948 m)
Coastline 250 mi (402 km)
Population 5,426,618
Major cities and populations
Freetown 822,000
Koidu 85,000
Ethnic groups
Temne, Mende, Limba, Koranko,
Religions
Traditional animism 30%, Islam
60%, Christianity 10%
Languages
English (official), indigenous
languages

ECONOMIC
Currency Leone
Industry
mining, beverages, textiles,
footwear, petroleum refining
Agriculture
wheat, barley, sugar cane, fruits,
beef cattle, sheep, wool, poultry,
dairy
Natural resources
diamonds, titanium ore, bauxite,
iron ore, gold, chromite

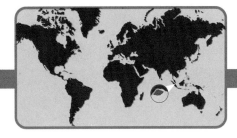

Singapore

REPUBLIC OF SINGAPORE

Just north of the equator, Singapore is made up of a main island and 50 small islets off the southern tip of the Malay peninsula. Singapore Island has a central area of low hills rising to an elevation of only 577 feet (176 meters). Coral reefs are found in the coastal areas. Numerous short streams drain the island. Most of the former jungle and swampland is now used for residential, industrial and agricultural purposes. A small area of the central hills are still forested. The country has a wet tropical climate. The climate is equatorial — hot and humid throughout the year. The rainy season occurs from November through January.

Singaporeans are almost all descended from immigrants. The largest ethnic group is the Chinese, who account for three-quarters of the population. Next largest is the Malays with approximately fifteen percent, then the Indians at seven percent. Nearly half of the people are Buddhists. The rest of the population is Christian, Muslim or Hindu. English, Mandarin, Malay and Tamil are all official languages.

Industry in Singapore has grown significantly since the 1960s. Its manufactures include office machinery, telecommunications equipment, chemicals, pharmaceuticals, electronic items, clothing, rubber products, steel pipes, plywood and processed foods. Shipbuilding and petroleum refining are also important. Singapore has become a leader in the development of biotechnology.

Relatively little farming is done in Singapore due to the

The statue of T. S. Raffles on the banks of the Singapore River.

SCOTT BRODIE

Singapore

Singapore's program of developing affordable housing for its citizens has been a major success.

small amount of arable land and the relatively poor soils. Fishing, largely from the port of Jurong, is significant to Singapore's economy.

Singapore is also renowned as a financial center for Asia. Its comprehensive legal structure and the reputation for integrity make Singapore an attractive place for such organizations to be located. More than thirty-five percent of the workforce is engaged in financial and business services.

Singapore has one of the highest standards of living of any country in Asia. It has complex systems of transportation and communication. Singapore's international airport is considered among the best in the world. High taxes and fees on motor vehicles help keep pollution problems well below those of other Asian nations.

Singapore is a republic with a parliament adapted from the British Westminster system. The head of state is the president, a largely ceremonial role, elected by popular vote for four years. Political power is in the hands of the prime minister and cabinet. Members of the unicameral legislature are elected for five-year terms.

Chinese immigrants had become established on the island they called Tumasik by the early fourteenth century. These people had difficulty sharing the island with gangs of pirates who raided trading ships heading for China.

Singapore became a trading center within the Sri Vijaya Empire, which was based in Sumatra. The Javanese Buddhist Majaphit empire went to war with Srivijaya in 1377. Much of Tumasik was destroyed.

Thomas Stamford Raffles became Lieutenant-Governor of Bencoolen (Bengkulu) in Sumatra on behalf of the British East India Company. He realized that Singapore's location on major shipping routes made it the ideal location for a trading port. Stamford landed at Singapore on January 29, 1819. He

negotiated a deal with the sultan of Johore, the local ruler.

Some enthusiastic promotion among the merchants of India and China established Singapore as a popular trading port within a very short time. Singapore, Malacca and Penang became the Straits Settlements, with their own governor, in 1826. British East India Company control ended in 1858, when the British government took direct control.

When Malaya began growing rubber during the 1870s, Singapore became the main port for the export of the rubber. The opening of the Suez Canal in 1869 created an increase in the number of ships stopping at Singapore. The resultant prosperity of Singapore attracted immigrants from other parts of Asia, particularly China. Although Europeans ran the

Parliament House.

large trading companies, day-to-day commerce was handled by Chinese merchants.

Successful merchants enjoyed an extravagant lifestyle with servants and large houses. Life for the people who worked for them was not good at all. As time passed, the gap between rich and poor widened.

Britain designated Singapore as its principal Asian naval base after World War I. It built extensive military facitilies on the island.

The Japanese Imperial Army captured Singapore on February 15, 1942. Tens of thousands of British, Australian and Indian troops were sent to prison camps across Asia. The Japanese renamed the island Syonan, or Light of the South.

Raffles Hotel has been a social center for Singapore for more than a century.

Britain liberated the island on September 6, 1945. The following year Singapore was made a separate crown colony. Britain established Singaporean Executive and Legislative Councils in 1947. Governors continued to be appointed from London. Six members of the Legislative Council were elected by the people in Singapore's first election on March 20, 1948.

The growing struggle between Britain and the communist movement for control of Singapore and Malaya led to the declaration of a state of emergency in the fall of 1948. Large numbers of British troops were stationed in Singapore.

A new constitution was adopted in 1955. David Marshall, leader of the Labor Front, was elected chief minister in a coalition government. Communist attempts to unseat Marshall's government led to bloody riots in the spring of 1955 after police broke up strikers' picket lines. Students joined in, protesting conditions in high schools. A threat to close the schools resulted in 2000 students barricading themselves inside Chung Cheng High School. After severe criticism of his handling of the events, Marshall resigned in 1956.

His replacement, Lim Yew Hok, deregistered communist-backed unions and the students' union. Student sit-ins exploded into bloody riots on October 25th. After five days under cur-

Singapore

few, thirteen people had died and hundreds were injured.

Britain agreed to further self-government and a new constitution in 1958. Singaporeans elected the People's Action Party (PAP), led by Lee Kuan Yew, to forty-three of the fifty-one parliamentary seats in 1959.

Many people believed Singapore should become united with Malaya. A referendum was held. The overwhelming majority favored union. Singapore, Malaya, British North Borneo (renamed Sabah) and Sarawak united to form Malaysia on September 16, 1963. Indonesia demonstrated its opposition to the union by exploding a bomb in a Singapore hotel eight days later.

Ethnic friction between the predominantly Chinese community of Singapore and the predominantly Malay community of Malaya shook the new nation. Fighting between cultural groups in Singapore erupted into full-scale race riots on July 21, 1964. Twenty-three people died. The Malaysian parliament approved Singapore's separation from the union in 1965.

Singapore was declared a republic and joined the United Nations later that year. It embarked on an ambitious plan of economic and social development. Singapore, Malaysia, Indonesia, the Philippines and

Thailand formed the Association of Southeast Asian Nations (ASEAN) in 1967.

Prime Minister Lee Kaun Yew held office from 1959 to 1990. His People's Action Party held the majority of parliaments seats during most of that time. Lee governed with a firm hand. He was a staunch supporter of U.S. policies in Southeast Asia. He wanted to curb Communist subversion.

Lee entered into a defense alliance with Australia, Great Britain, Malaysia and New Zealand in 1971. After the end of the Vietnam War, he adopted a more conciliatory attitude toward Communist regimes in the area. He finally extended diplomatic recognition to China in 1990. Lee resigned in 1990 and designated Goh Chok Tong as his successor. Goh Chok Tong remains in office.

Singapore has made great strides since it became a republic. The energy of a diverse ethnicity has worked much to its favor. The people work effectively in a single-minded drive to create a better life for everyone. International companies established manufacturing plants in Singapore, creating jobs and new opportunities. Many Singaporean industries began marketing their goods and services around the world.

A massive housing development program provides better living quarters for Singapore's poor. Many slums have been cleared. People were relocated into modern dwellings in various areas across the island.

The worldwide economic slump of the late 1990s has had its effect on Singapore. Demand for its goods, particularly electronics, had decreased by the beginning of the 2000s. Singapore's economy remains among the strongest in Asia nonetheless. The People's Action Party again dominated the 2001 elections.

The colonial-era Cricket Club is dwarfed by commercial towers.

Slovakia

SLOVAK REPUBLIC

Landlocked Slovakia is located in central Europe between Poland and Hungary. The Carpathian Mountains run for most of the length of the border with Poland. The Danube River forms part of the border with Hungary and Austria. The fertile lowlands east of the Danube are an extension of the plain of Hungary. The climate is continental with minimal rainfall during the cold winters. In summer, temperatures are warm with heavy rainfall.

Eighty-five percent of the population is ethnically Slovak and ten percent is Hungarian. There are small Gypsy and Czech minorities. Slovakia is predominantly Roman Catholic. Protestants and Orthodox religions account for a large part of the remainder. Slovak is the official language.

Slovakia's manufacturing industries offer processed foods, textiles, chemicals, plastics, refined metals, household appliances, fertilizers and armaments. Much of the country's agriculture takes place in southern regions near the Danube. Wheat, potatoes, beet sugar, barley, hops and fruits are the main crops. Coal, lignite, copper, lead, zinc and iron ore are extensively mined.

Slovakia's constitution was adopted in 1993. The National Council is a unicameral parliament with members elected to four-year terms by popular vote based on proportional representation. The president is elected directly by the people for a five-year term. The president appoints the prime minister, who is usually the majority leader of the National Council. The president also appoints a cabinet on the recommendation of the prime minister.

Slavik tribes settled the region now known as Slovakia in the fifth century. Slovakia came under the dominance of the kingdom of Moravia in the ninth century. The Moravians introduced Christianity. Slovakia came under Hungarian control after the assault on the Moravians by the Magyars early in the eleventh century.

The Ottoman Turks defeated the Hungarians at Mohács in 1526. Slovakia was absorbed into the Habsburg Empire as part of Royal Hungary. The Slovak city of Bratislava became the Habsburg capital until the late 1600s. Habsburg nobles acquired much of Slovakia's prime land.

The Habsburgs stepped up the Germanization of Slovakia during the eighteenth century. A new nationalism spread across the land, influenced by similar movements in Hungary and the Czech region. Anti-Habsburg uprisings occurred in 1848 with demands for increased cultural and political rights. Large numbers of Slovaks emigrated to the United States at the

GOVERNMENT
Website
www.government.gov.sk/english
Capital Bratislava
Type of government Republic
Separation from Czechoslovakia
January 1, 1993
Voting
Universal adult suffrage, compulsory
Head of state President
Head of government Prime Minister
Constitution 1992
Legislature
Unicameral National Council
Judiciary Supreme Court
Member of CE, IMF, OECD, UN, UNESCO, WHO, WTO

LAND AND PEOPLE
Land area 18,933 sq mi
(49,036 sq km)
Highest point Gerlachovka
8,711 ft (2,655 m)
Population 5,414,937
Major cities and populations
Bratislava 875,000
Kosice 250,000
Zilina 190,000
Ethnic groups Slovak 85%,
Hungarian 10%
Religions Christianity
Languages
Slovak (official), Czech, Hungarian

ECONOMIC
Currency Slovak koruna
Industry
metal products, food, beverages, mining, nuclear fuel, chemicals, artificial fibres, machinery, paper, ceramics, motor vehicles, textiles, optical apparatus, rubber products
Agriculture
grains, potatoes, beet sugar, hops, fruit, pigs, cattle, poultry, timber
Natural resources
brown coal, lignite, iron ore, copper, manganese, salt

Slovakia

beginning of the twentieth century.

The Austro-Hungarian monarchy ended after World War I. Slovaks joined with Czechs to create Czechoslovakia in October of 1918. The union was fraught with difficulties for decades. Slovaks were never happy with power being concentrated in Prague, the Czech capital. The Czech people outnumbered the Slovaks.

The new country also had a large minority of ethnic Germans. The Sudeten German Party arose. Under Konrad Henlein, it demanded more autonomy for Germans in Czechoslavia. The Munich Agreement of 1938 laid out a rearrangement of the country, giving more power to the Germans. Part of Slovakia went to Hungary and part of it became an independent state.

The new Slovakia came under the control of Father Joseph Tiso. Tiso was a puppet and military ally of the German Third Reich. A vigorous World War II resistance movement against the Tiso regime was supported by the Soviet Union.

Communists, backed by the Soviet Union, set up a new Czechoslovakia Republic at the end of World War II. Slovakia rejoined the union.

Industry, commerce, and transporation were all nationalized under the new government. Churches were attacked and restricted. Cultural and educational activities were revamped in keeping with the Communist viewpoint.

A reformist government under the leadership of Alexander Dubcek came to power in January of 1968. A new federal constitution was drafted to greatly liberalize the country.The USSR, aided by a coalition of other countries, sent 600,000 troops to crush the Dubcek government in August. Despite this, the new federation came into effect on January 1, 1969. The country became a separate Communist state.

The collapse of Soviet communism in 1989 led Slovaks to agitate for independence and nationhood. Czechoslovakia suffered considerably during the early 1990s as it changed to a market economy.

The Czechs and the Slovaks failed to agree on a new constitution. The federal parliament voted to divide Czechoslovakia into two independent nations in November of 1992. Slovakia came into being on January 1, 1993, with Vladimir Meciar as prime minister. Parliament elected Michael Kovac as president of the republic.

Privatization of industry continues to cause problems for Slovakia. Dissatisfaction with economic progress is widespread. Inflation remained high into the 2000s, but the economy seems to be improving.

The old Town Hall in Bratislava, Slovakia's capital.

Slovenia

REPUBLIC OF SLOVENIA

A former republic of Yugoslavia, Slovenia is located in southeastern Europe. Most of the country lies within the Karst plateau and the Julian Alps. The only coastline is a tiny strip on the Adriatic Sea. The Drava and Sava rivers flow south into Croatia. Slovenia's climate is Mediterranean near the Adriatic Sea, whereas in the mountainous inland it is continental.

Ethnic Slovenes comprise ninety percent of the population. Christianity, largely Catholicism, prevails throughout the country. There is a small Muslim minority. Most people speak Slovenian.

Illyrian and Celtic tribes were the earliest inhabitants of Slovenia. It became part of the Roman Empire during the first century B.C. Slavs arrived in the sixth century A.D., establishing the state of Samo.

A period of domination by Bavaria followed. Most people converted to Roman Catholicism during this time. The region became part of the Frankish Empire in the late eighth century. It was reorganized as a duchy of the Holy Roman Empire in the tenth century.

Most of Slovenia came under the control of the Austrian Habsburg dynasty during the thirteenth and fourteenth centuries. Austrian culture spread throughout the land.

The region was taken from Austria by France during the Napoleonic Wars of 1809 - 1814. It was reorganized as the Illyrian provinces. A period of liberal rule followed. The Slovenes' spirit of nationalism grew rapidly. The Slovene People's Party was formed in the 1890s.

The Kingdom of Serbs, Croats and Slovenes was founded at the end of World War I in 1918. The country was renamed the Kingdom of Yugoslavia in 1929.

Slovenia was divided among Italy, Germany and Hungary in 1941. Slovenia once again became part of Yugoslavia at the end of World War II. Most ethnic Slovenes remained in the Slovenian republic. Slovenian culture flowered in the following years. Industries, including tourism, developed and flourished.

The Slovenian parliament issued a proclamation of independence in June of 1991. This helped trigger a Yugoslav civil war. Slovenia became fully independent on October 8, 1991. Slovenia joined the United Nations in May of 1992. Large-scale privatization of industry provoked strikes and demands from civil servants for pay increases. Economic stability was aided by substantial foreign investment. Iron, steel, motor vehicle, chemical and textile industries were all growing rapidly by the 2000s.

Solomon Islands

The Solomon Islands is an archipelago in the southwestern Pacific Ocean, northeast of Australia. It is made up of six large islands, over 100 smaller ones and numerous atolls. The large islands were originated by volcanoes. They are mountainous, with dense rainforest covering. The climate is equatorial, with high temperatures throughout the year.

Ninety percent of Solomon Islanders are Melanesian. There are some Polynesians on the smaller islands. The people are predominantly Christian. The majority belong to the Anglican or Catholic churches. English is the official language, although Pidgin English and other local dialects are widely spoken.

Melanesian people have lived in the Solomon Islands since 1000 B.C. Spanish explorer Alvaro de Mendana named the region after King Solomon in A.D.1568. European traders and missionaries arrived during the nineteenth century. Palm oil cultivation soon became a primary industry.

Germany took control of the northern islands in 1885. They transferred all of the islands, except for Bougainville and Buca, to the British in 1900. Britain had already declared a protectorate over the central and southern islands in 1893.

Australia occupied Bougainville and Buca during World War I. Those islands later became part of Papua New Guinea.

Guadalcanal Island was the scene of a massive battle between Allied and Japanese forces during World War II. Japan was forced to vacate the islands after the war.

The Solomon Islands became independent on July 7, 1978, within the Commonwealth of Nations. Peter Kenilorea was the first prime minister.

The years since independence have been marked by consistent economic, political and ethnic struggles. Excessive logging of native forests led Australia to reduce its foreign aid.

Violence erupted on Guadalcanal when local militants attacked immigrants from the island of Malaita in the late 1990s. About sixty people were killed, while more than 20,000 had to flee their homes. Peace talks progressed very slowly. An October 2000 agreement was ignored by many of the militants, who still control much of the countryside.

The upheaval on Guadalcanal had serious effects on the Solomon Islands' already weak economy. Some businesses were temporarily shut down. Many others were permanently closed. Unemployment continued to rise. The situation remains highly unstable.

GOVERNMENT
Website www.solomons.com
Capital Honiara
Type of government Parliamentary democracy
Independence from Britain July 7, 1978
Voting Universal adult suffrage, compulsory
Head of state British Crown, represented by Governor-General
Head of government Prime Minister
Constitution 1978
Legislature Unicameral Parliament
Judiciary Court of Appeal
Member of CN, IMF, SPF, UN, UNESCO, WHO, WTO

LAND AND PEOPLE
Land area 10,954 sq mi (28,370 sq km)
Highest point Mt. Makarakomburu 8,028 ft (2,447 m)
Coastline 3,301 mi (5,313 km)
Population 480,442
Major cities and populations Honiara 68,000
Ethnic groups Melanesian 90%, Polynesian 5%, Micronesian 2%, European 1%, others 2%
Religions Christianity
Languages English (official), Pidgin, indigenous languages

ECONOMIC
Currency Solomon Islands dollar
Industry fisheries, mining, timber
Agriculture cacao, beans, coconuts, palm kernels, rice, potatoes, vegetables, fruit, cattle, pigs, timber
Natural resources seafood, forests, gold, bauxite, phosphates, lead, zinc, nickel

Somalia

SOMALI DEMOCRATIC REPUBLIC

Somalia is located in the Horn of northeastern Africa, with coastlines on the Indian Ocean and the Gulf of Aden. Much of the landscape is semi-arid desert. Sandy, infertile coastal plains rise to an inland plateau and mountains. Little rain falls and drought is commonplace. Temperatures are generally high.

Ninety percent of the population belongs to five distinct Somali clans. Bantu people are found in the southwest. Other minorities include Arabs, Indisans, Italians and Pakistanis. Virtually all the population is Sunni Muslim. Somali and Arabic are the official languages.

The area of Somalia belonged to the Ethiopian kingdom of Aksum from the second to the seventh centuries A.D. Arab tribes settled along the Gulf of Aden coast, where they established the sultantate of Aden in the seventh century. Somali people from Yemen migrated to the region in the thirteen century. Islam became widespread during this time.

Britain established the Somaliland protectorate in 1887. Italy wrote treaties with native Somali tribes to gain substantial economic power and eventual control of the country. Italian troops expelled the British during World War II. Britain recaptured it in 1941.

A peace treaty signed in 1947 specified that Somaliland would be adminstered by Italy for ten years as a U.N. trust territory. The United Republic of Somalia was established on July 1, 1960.

Following President Abdi-Rashid Ali Shermarke's assassination in 1969, Major General Mohammed Siyad Barre became president. He declared the country a socialist state. Most of the economy of the Somalia was nationalized.

Ethnic Somalis in the Ogaden region of Ethiopia rebelled against Ethiopian control. The Somali army suffered heavy losses at the hands of the Ethiopians, who were aided by the USSR. Close to two million people fled Ethiopia to Somalia. The U.S. provided humanitarian and military aid.

Barre was deposed in 1991. About 50,000 people were killed in subsequent fighting, while a additional 300,000 died of starvation. International agencies resumed food distribution. U.N. peacekeepers tried, in vain, to bring warring factions to an accord.

Floods in southern Somalia killed 1,400 people and left 230,000 homeless in 1999. Fighting continued in many of the southern and central areas. Severe food shortages persisted in many areas.

A conference of Somali peace activists met in Djibouti in 2000. An interim parliament was elected. Abdikassam Salad Hassan was named president.

South Africa

REPUBLIC OF SOUTH AFRICA

South Africa is in the far south of the African continent. Its east coast fronts the Indian Ocean, while its west coast faces the Atlantic Ocean. Around the coast is a narrow, fertile strip of low land. Dominating the inland is the African Plateau, stretching north to the Kalahari Desert. In the east and northeast is the Great Escarpment, rising beyond an elevation of 11,115 feet (3,400 meters) in the Drakensberg Range. The primary waterway is the Orange River system which empties into the Atlantic.

Most of the country is subtropical. Coastal areas are affected by the Mozambique and Benguela currents. The former promotes heavy rainfall and lush vegetation on the northeastern coast. The latter, moving north from the Antarctic, creates a drier climate in the west. The coast has cool winters and warm summers. The interior experiences cool to cold winters and much hotter summers. It has much lower humidity than the coast.

Seventy-five percent of South Africans are of African descent. The major ethnic groups are the Xhosa, Tswana, Sotho, Zulu, Swazi, Venda, Pedi, Tsonga and Ndebele. Europeans make up about fourteen percent of the population. A large group of mixed race people, mostly of European, Indian and Malay heritage, numbers eight percent. Asian people account for three percent.

Most South Africans are Christian. About eight percent follow traditional indigenous beliefs. Hinduism is practiced mainly in the Indian community, and there is a significant Muslim minority.

South Africa has eleven official languages: English, Afrikaans, Zulu, Sotho, Tswana, Xhosa, Swazi, Venda, Ndebele, Pedi and Tsonga. Gujurati, Hindi, Urdu and Tamil are spoken in the Asian communities.

The government of South Africa practiced apartheid for many years. This involved the separation of races in most aspects of life. Homelands were developed to divide the various peoples by race. Apartheid was abolished in 1994. The country is now working to become a

FLAT EARTH PICTURE GALLERY

Johannesburg's central business district.

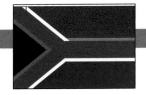

nation of diversity, acceptance and equality.

The economy of South Africa grew from the end of World War II, but it started to decline in the 1970s. International economic sanctions aimed at ending discriminatory racial policies did considerable damage during the 1980s. Apartheid has now ended, but the nation's wealth remains predominantly in the hands of the whites. Unemployment among black South Africans is very high.

Mining plays a large part in South Africa's economy. Major products of South Africa's mines include gold, platinum, iron ore, diamonds, coal, copper, nickel, tin, uranium, vanadium, chromium, fluorite, phosphates, salt and lime. Large amounts of oil and gas

are produced synthetically from coal. Forestry and fishing also play an important part in South Africa's economy.

Manufacturing has had a growing importance since World War II. Learding manufactures include machinery, chemicals, transportation equipment, textiles, clothing, paper, tobacco products, processed foods and beverages.

The lack of suitable land means agriculture plays only a minor role in the economy. About 85 percent of all suitable farmland is used for raising livestock. Farms produce nearly all of the crops needed for the country's residents.

South Africa's 1996 constitution was formulated following

Waiting for a bus in downtown Johannesburg.

GOVERNMENT
Website www.gov.za
Capital Pretoria
Type of government Republic
Independence from Britain
May 3, 1910 (dominion status)
Voting Universal adult suffrage
Head of state and government
President
Constitution 1996
Legislature
Bicameral Parliament
National Assembly (lower house),
National Council of Provinces
(upper house)
Judiciary Constitutional Court
Member of CN, IMF, UN,
UNESCO, UNHCR, WHO, WTO

LAND AND PEOPLE
Land area 470,690 sq mi
(1,219,080 sq km)
Highest point Njesuthi
11,181 ft (3,408 m)
Coastline 1,738 mi (2,798 km)
Population 43,586,097
Major cities and populations
Cape Town 2.9 million
Johannesburg 2.4 million
Pretoria 1.5 million
Ethnic groups
African 75%, European 14%
Religions Christianity, indigenous
beliefs, Islam, Hinduism
Languages Eleven official
languages, including English and
Afrikaans

ECONOMIC
Currency Rand
Industry
mining, motor vehicles, machinery,
textiles, iron, steel, chemicals,
fertilizer, processed foods
Agriculture corn, wheat, sugar
cane, fruits, vegetables, livestock
Natural resources
gold, chromium, antimony, coal,
iron ore, manganese, nickel,
phosphates, tin, uranium,
diamonds, platinum, copper,
vanadium, salt, natural gas

FLAT EARTH PICTURE GALLERY

South Africa

the end of apartheid and the introduction of universal adult suffrage. The nation is a federal republic. The president, as head of state and head of government, is elected for a five-year term by the members of the National Assembly. The parliament is bicameral. The National Assembly, or lower house, is elected by a proportional representation system. The upper house, the National Council, is elected by the nine provincial legislatures.

San people roamed the area of South Africa as hunters and gatherers during the Stone Age. Khoikhoi people colonized the southern coast about 2,000 years ago. Bantu-speaking peoples settled in northern areas beginning in the eighth century A.D. They mined gold and copper.

The Dutch East India Company established a settlement at Table Bay on the Cape of Good Hope in 1652. Dutch and French settlers arrived, displacing the native Khoikhoi people. Cape Town became a major port as a way station for East Indies trade.

The East India Company demanded all arrivals adopt the Dutch language and follow the Dutch Reformed Church. These colonists, most of whom were farmers or cattle herders, became known as Boers. They developed a hybrid language called Afrikaans.

FLAT EARTH PICTURE GALLERY

The imperial grandeur of Cape Town's Civic Hall.

Through the eighteenth century, the Boers moved further inland, forcing more of the Khoikhoi off their lands. The San were driven north. Competition for land among native tribes later led to wars in which thousands perished.

Britain occupied the Cape region beginning in 1795. They purchased the Cape Colony from the Dutch in 1814. More than 5,000 British migrants arrived in 1820, taking up land around the Great Fish River. Few remained there; most moved to the towns. This was the first European group not absorbed into Afrikaner culture. The British imposed their own law and made English the official language. They instituted protection for the Khoikhoi people and they abolished slavery.

Afrikaner peoples were dissatisfied with British control, especially the abolition of slavery. They began trekking north into regions previously unclaimed by Europeans. Against fierce Zulu resistance, they established the Orange Free State, and the Transvaal and Natal territories.

The British soon established Natal as a crown colony in 1843. Afrikaners left Natal and formed the Orange Free State and the Transvaal republics. The British recognized the independence of the Transvaal regions and the Orange Free State in the 1850s. Areas beyond the Vaal River formed the South African Republic by the late 1850s.

Diamonds were discovered in Griqualand West, part of the South African Republic, in 1867. Britain decided to press into this territory, declaring Basutoland (now Lesotho) a protectorate and reimposing British rule over the South African Republic. Afrikaners took up arms against the British in 1881. The South African Republic was allowed a degree of independence.

Cecil Rhodes was premier of the Cape Colony and a prominent British business leader. He wanted control of the Witwatersrand and Orange Free State gold mines discovered in 1886. He encouraged anti-Boer feelings among mine workers. He staged a raid, led by Leander Starr Jameson, in late 1895. It was intended to signal an uprising of mine workers.

Britain demanded Orange Free State become a British colony. Its leader, Paul Kruger, refused. This launched the South African, or Boer, War, in 1899. Kruger's forces attacked Natal and the Cape Colony. They were initially successful, besieging British forces at Mafeking, Kimberley and Ladysmith.

Large numbers of troops poured in from Britain, Australia, New Zealand and elsewhere. British commanders used the controversial method of collecting civilian Boer sympathizers in concentration camps.

Transvaal and Orange Free State were incorporated into the British Empire under the 1902 Treaty of Vereeniging. Britain passed the South Africa Act in May 1910, establishing the Union of South Africa as a British dominion. The South African Party won the first elections. Former Boer army commander, Louis Botha, became prime minister.

South African troops captured German South West Africa (Namibia) in 1915. The League of Nations made it a South African mandated territory five years later.

J. B. Hertzog became prime minister in 1924. Afrikaner culture became dominant under his leadership. A steady progression of laws enhanced the dominance of the European minority. Jan Christiaan Smuts became prime minister in 1939. He sent troops to support Britain in World War II.

The National Party gained power in 1948. D. F. Malan became prime minister. This marked the beginning of the racist policy of apartheid. It officially separated Europeans and Africans into separate cultures and geographical areas. Europeans benefited most.

Stallholders selling fruit in Johannesburg.

They had the best land, the best jobs and economic control.

Apartheid was strengthened by a succession of new laws. Marriages between Europeans and Africans were banned in 1949. Europeans could move around the country unhindered, but Africans had to have passes to enter certain areas. This was the key to controlling the African population and suppressing uprisings.

The U.N. Security Council condemned apartheid in 1964. It later voted to terminate South Africa's control of South West Africa. Years of fighting ensued until, in 1988, South West Africa was granted its independence as Namibia.

South Africa

Opponents of the government, most notably Nelson Mandela, were imprisoned during the 1960s. South Africa withdrew from the Commonwealth of Nations, following condemnation by other member states. It became a republic in 1961.

Most other African nations severed diplomatic relations with South Africa. Use of African air space was denied to South African airlines. Its aircraft were forced to fly out over the Atlantic, skirting the continent to reach Europe.

Enlightened European South Africans were challenging the hard-line National Party policies by the 1970s. Some 10,000 students in the township of Soweto protested the enforced use of Afrikaans, in addition to English, in their schools. This prompted further riots, arson, and killing in Soweto, which soon spread to many other places. The next year black leader Steve Biko was beaten to death while in police custody.

Four African homelands, called bantustaans, were developed in the 1970s. Although independent, there was little doubt they would be crushed if they diverted from South African policy.

The early 1980s saw military anti-guerrilla incursions into neighboring states. A tricameral parliament inaugurated in 1984 had separate houses for

Harvesting wine grapes at Stellenbosch.

Europeans, Africans and Coloureds, the name given to those of mixed heritage. Violent protests by the African community led to a state of emergency in 1985.

President P. W. Botha was replaced by F. W. de Klerk in 1989. De Klerk began easing the apartheid laws. The African National Congress (ANC), outlawed for thirty years, was legalized. Its leader, Nelson Mandela, was released from his long imprisonment in 1990.

A constitutional convention led to a March 1992 referendum of the European population. They endorsed multiracial democracy by a large majority. European and African extremists opposed the process. Zulus, led by Chief Mangosuthu Buthelezi, tried to disrupt the change. The Afrikaner Resistance Movement pledged to reinstate apartheid.

An interim constitution was established in 1993. The following year South Africa held its first multiracial election. The ANC won easily and Mandela became president. The last remnants of apartheid were swept away by 1995. South Africa rejoined the Commonwealth of Nations.

Such sweeping changes required huge efforts to keep the economy on track. Fortu-

nately, the ANC and Mandela had massive public support.

The Truth and Reconciliation Commission, led by Archbishop Desmond Tutu, was formed in 1996. It proceeded to document the human rights abuses which occurred under apartheid.

The quality of life for many Africans has improved enormously. Unfortunately, the crime rate has risen dramatically. Thabo Mbeki succeeded Mandela as president in 1999. He does not enjoy the devotion and respect shown Mandela. Mbeki has been credited for expanding South Africa's economic and political influence. Western nations have applauded his emphasis on attracting foreign investment rather than financial aid.

Spain

KINGDOM OF SPAIN

Spain occupies eighty percent of the Iberian Peninsula in southwestern Europe. The Balearic Islands in the Mediterranean Sea and the Canary Islands in the Atlantic Ocean are also part of Spain. Spain also administers two small enclaves on the coast of Morocco in northern Africa. The center of the country is a large plateau called the Meseta. The plateau is divided into northern and southern sections by irregular mountain ranges. The largest of these are the Sierra de Guadarrama, the Sierra de Gredos and the Montes de Toledo. The Pyrenees range forms a natural border with France in the northeast. Spain's coastline extends from the border with France, southwest along the Mediterranean to the Strait of Gibraltar. It then continues along the Atlantic coast to the border with Portugal. The northern coast faces the Bay of Biscay.

Climatic conditions vary greatly. The central plateau experiences a continental climate, with cold winters and warm summers. The climate is Mediterranean along the southern coast, with warm winters and hot summers. Rainfall is heavy in the mountain regions.

Most of the population is ethnically Spanish. There are a number of separate cultural groups, such as the Basques and the Catalans. These groups are different primarily in the languages they speak. About two percent of the people are nomadic Gypsies. Expatriates from other parts of Europe have made their homes in Spain, mostly in resort areas.

Most of the people are Christians, predominantly Catholics. There is a small Muslim minority.

Castilian Spanish is the official language. It is spoken by about three-quarters of the population. The people of the Balearics, Catalonia and Valencia speak Catalan. Many people of the northwest speak Galician. Basque is widely spoken in the northeast.

Spain is one of largest producers of agricultural commodities in western Europe. Major agricultural crops are beet sugar, barley, tomatoes, wheat, grapes, olives, citrus fruits and cork. Large numbers of livestock, particularly sheep and goats, are raised on Spanish farms. The upper Ebro valley and Andalusia are home to Spain's large wine industry. Spain is Europe's largest producer of lemons, oranges and strawberries. It is the world's largest producer of olive oil.

Spain's industries have grown rapidly since the 1950s. Heavy manufactures include motor vehicles, diesel engines and various types of machinery. Lighter manufacturing

GOVERNMENT
Website www.la-moncloa.es
Capital Madrid
Type of government
Constitutional monarchy
Voting Universal adult suffrage
Head of state Monarch
Head of government
Prime minister
Constitution 1978
Legislature
Bicameral General Courts
Congress of Deputies (lower house),
Senate (upper house)
Judiciary Supreme Court
Member of CE, EU, IMF, NATO, OECD, UN, UNESCO, UNHCR, WHO, WTO

LAND AND PEOPLE
Land area 194,897 sq mi (504,782 sq km)
Highest point Pico de Teide 12,198 ft (3,718 m)
Coastline 3,084 mi (4,964 km)
Population 40,037,995
Major cities and populations
Madrid 4 million
Barcelona 2.8 million
Valencia 0.8 million
Ethnic groups
Spanish 98%, Gypsy 2%
Religions Christianity 97%, Islam 1%
Languages Castilian Spanish (official), Basque, Catalan, Galician

ECONOMIC
Currency Euro
Industry
textiles, garments, footwear beverages, chemicals, shipbuilding, motor vehicles, machine tools
Agriculture
grain, vegetables, olives, wine grapes, beet sugar, citrus, beef, pork, poultry, dairy,
Natural resources
coal, lignite, iron ore, uranium, mercury, pyrites, fluorspar, gypsum, zinc, lead, tungsten, copper, kaolin, potash

Spain

produces appliances, electrical equipment, footwear and textiles. There is also a substantial processed food industry. Canning of fish, including cod, anchovies and tuna, is vital to the economy of the Atlantic coast region.

The largest mines are found in the Cordillera Cantábrica. Iron, zinc and coal are extracted. Copper, lead, tin, silver and mercury are mined in other parts of the country. There are oilfields around Burgos, but Spain is not a major producer.

Tourism is a massive industry. Millions of visitors flock to the beach resorts along the southeastern coastline, particularly during winter months. The Balearic and Canary islands are also popular. Spain's cities, countryside and cultural heritage are popular attractions.

Spain underwent a political transformation in the late 1970s. The authoritarian regime of Francisco Franco was replaced by a restored monarchy and an influential parliament. Spain's monarch holds office for life, having inherited the position. The monarchy nominates the prime minister for approval by the parliament. The prime minister is voted

The dramatic splendor of Gaudi's Sagrada Familia church in Barcelona.

into office by the Congress of Deputies. Power is also vested in a cabinet, or council of ministers. The Council of State is an consultive body.

The bicameral parliament, consists of the Chamber of Deputies and the Senate. Members of both houses are popularly elected for four-year terms. The prime minister, officially called President of the Government, is a member of the Chamber of Deputies. Each of Spain's autonomous regions has its own elected parliament.

People have lived in Spain since the Stone Age. Remains include the cave paintings in the Altamira region. A unique people called the Iberians inhabited the region by about 2000 B.C. Celts crossed the Pyrenees to mix with the Iberians a thousand years later. Phoenician traders from the eastern Mediterranean reached the Spanish coast soon afterward. They established trading settlements in Andalusia and the Balearic Islands.

The peninsula was invaded by the Carthaginians from north Africa during the third century B.C. They established a capital at Cartagena under the leadership of Hamilcar Barca. The region became part of the Roman Empire after the Second Punic War between Carthage and Rome.

The Romans quickly took eastern and southern Spain,

An Andalusian dancer.

but they spent almost two centuries gaining control of the north. Roman culture was quickly embraced by the local people. The orderly Roman administrative structure generated considerable economic prosperity.

Spain was invaded by Germanic tribes as Rome's power waned. First came the Suevi, then the Vandals and finally the Visigoths. The Visigoths expelled the Vandals. They established a kingdom covering southern Gaul and much of Spain by A.D.419. Visigoth King Alaric II was deposed by the king of the Franks in 507 and until 554 Spain was part of the Frankish Empire. The Visigoths regained southern Spain and moved their capital to Toledo.

Christianity was introduced in the first century A.D. It quickly gained a substantial hold on the population, existing side by side with paganism. King Recarred I converted to Christianity in 587 and declared Roman Catholicism the state religion. Jews were also playing an important role in Spanish civilization by this time. Christian dominance led to widespread persecution of the Jewish population in the seventh century.

The clash between Christianity, paganism and Judaism weakened the power of the

BRAND X PICTURES

Visigoth monarchs. Their control was shattered in 711. The Moors, a Berber people from north Africa, invaded Spain and swept across the land. Visigoth King Roderick was defeated by the Muslim armies of Tarik ibn Ziyad. The Moors controlled all but the northern portion of the Iberian Peninsula within a short time.

Spain

The harbour at Las Palmas in the Canary Islands.

BRAND X PICTURES

Moorish Spain was ruled under the authority of the Caliphate of Baghdad, with a capital at Córdoba. The independent Ummayad Caliphate of Córdoba was established in 756, under the rulership of Abd-dar-Rahman I.

The Umayyad dynasty ruled Muslim Spain for nearly 300 hundred years. Abd-dar Rahman III, its strongest ruler, declared himself caliph in 929. His capital of Córdoba was one of the most magnificent cities in Europe. He encouraged the arts and sciences. Literature and architecture flourished.

The Ummayyad dynasty ended shortly after the death of Hisham III in 1036. Various small kingdoms formed, the most prominent being Córdoba. The Almoravids gradually took control of Moorish Spain. They were displaced in 1145 by the Almohads. Christian kings from the north advanced on the Moors. They fought a great battle on the plains of Toledo in 1212. The Almohads were defeated by the united Christian powers. Moors were confined to Cadiz and the kingdom of Granada by the late thirteenth century.

Through royal marriages, conquest and inheritance, Castile and Aragón became the dominant kingdoms by the fifteenth century. Both had a diverse population of Christians, Muslims and Jews. .

Isabella, Princess of Castile, married Ferdinand, King of Aragón in 1469. They became joint rulers of the two kingdoms, instituting new laws and systems for government.

The expulsion of the Moors was completed in 1492 when Granada was captured. Spanish art, architecture and learning had reached a high point under the Moors. They had developed flourishing trade links with much of Europe. A prosperous steel industry had been built at Toledo, while a silk industry thrived at Granada.

Muslims had lived in relative peace with Christians prior to this time. Tolerance declined as Christianity became more dominant. The Catholic Church launched a campaign of intimidation against non-Christians and anyone who dissented from the established teachings in 1478. This was called the Spanish Inquisition. Jews and Muslims were forced to convert to Christianity by torture or persecution. Many Jews fled the country, taking their valuable commercial links with them.

Spain began its exploration and conquest of many parts of the world. Christopher Columbus reached the Americas. Ferdinand Magellan's expedition was the first to circumnavigate the world.

Spain and Portugal concluded the Treaty of Tordesillas in 1494. This agreement divided the areas to the west, including many places not yet discovered, between the two countries. Military forces called conquistadores, led by Hernando Cortés and Francisco

Pizarro, landed in South America. They began annexing territories that could produce new riches, particularly gold and silver. They rampaged through Central and South America, destroying civilizations such as those of the Aztecs of Mexico and the Incas of Peru.

Spain controlled most of the South American continent, Central America, Florida and Cuba by the 1550s. On the other side of the world, it annexed the islands it called the Philippines. The empire carried Christianity across the Atlantic. The conquests provided regular shipments of gold and silver to Spain.

King Ferdinand died in 1516. His successor was Charles I, a member of the Austrian Habsburg dynasty. Charles was crowned Holy Roman Emperor in 1519.

At this time, Spain was a collection of separate kingdoms, with Charles as the ultimate monarch. There were also numerous independent cities. Charles began a campaign to centralize authority under one monarch. His radical changes provoked an uprising by the cities in 1520–21. He abdicated in favor of his son Philip II in 1556, after centralization of the monarchy was complete.

The Spanish Inquisition reached the peak of its power and influence under Philip. Philip brought neighboring Portugal under Spanish control in 1580. The Spanish Empire was vast by this time. Its massive navy sailed most of the world's oceans.

The Protestant Reformation, which swept through northern Europe in the sixteenth century, was vigorously opposed by Spain. The Spanish Netherlands revolted and its northern half became independent in 1581.

Philip had married Britain's Queen Mary, daughter of King Henry VIII. When she died in 1558 without producing an heir, relations with England deteriorated. Mary's successor, Elizabeth I of England, promoted the Protestant Church. English pirates and privateers caused havoc by capturing Spanish

property in the Americas. Philip assembled a vast naval fleet, called the Armada, in 1588. The Armada was sent to invade England. It was soon defeated by the British fleet. The whole expedition was an enormous failure in terms of deaths and ships lost.

Spain, under Philip III and Philip IV, was drawn into the Thirty Years War in the early 1600s. France, although Catholic, supported the Protestants in this war. Conflict with France continued until 1659. The 1648 Peace of Westphalia made France Europe's dominant power, while the fortunes of Spain declined.

Portugal rebelled against Spanish control and regained its independence in 1640. Spanish provinces seeking greater automomy caused serious divisions within the country. The once great Spanish maritime

Taking a more leisurely pace in rural Spain.

FLAT EARTH PICTURE GALLERY

Spain

fleet was now trailing behind those of the Netherlands and Britain.

King Charles II, who ruled from 1665 to 1700, did not produce an heir. Many people started vying for power as the king neared the end of his life. Both France and Austria wanted to supply the new monarch and so secure control of Spain. Charles ultimately nominated the grandson of King Louis XIV of France as his successor. Britain, the Netherlands, Austria, Prussia and other countries formed a coalition opposed to a French monarch. This launched the War of the Spanish Succession, which lasted until 1714.

The Peace of Utrecht confirmed Philip V as King of Spain following a French victory. The Spanish Netherlands, Milan, Naples and Sardinia were handed over to the Austrian Habsburgs.

French influence over Spain increased for the rest of the eighteenth century. Following his 1799 coup in France, Napoleon Bonaparte moved to bring Spain under his control. Spain supported France's bid to conquer Portugal. Additional French troops were sent to

Spain's Moorish heritage is reflected in the magnificent Alhambra Museum in the Granada region.

Spain, supposedly as reinforcements for Portugal. They conquered Madrid in early 1808. A palace revolt in March deposed Spain's King Charles IV, replacing him with Ferdinand VII.

Napoleon forced Ferdinand's abdication in favor of his brother, Joseph Bonaparte in May of 1808. A violent uprising in Madrid was swiftly suppressed by French forces. Further revolts across the country forced Joseph to leave Madrid in August.

A British military force, commanded by General Arthur Wellesley, landed in Portugal the same month. The battle between Britain and France raged across Spain from 1809 to 1812. Many Spaniards aided the British forces. Wellesley pushed the French back into France in June of 1812. Most of Spain's colonies, particularly in South America, declared their independence during this time. Only Cuba and Puerto Rico remained.

Ferdinand VII was restored to the throne in 1814. He returned under the terms of a constitution drawn up in 1812 by Spain's first national parliament, the Cortes. It restricted the power of the monarch and ended the Inquisition. Ferdinand's persistent refusal to honor the constitution led to a revolt in 1820. It was put down by French forces at the monarch's request.

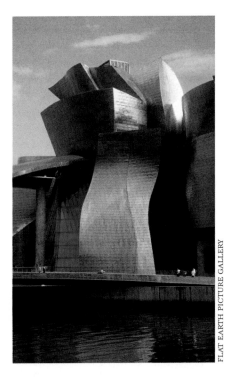

Before his death Ferdinand appointed his daughter Isabella II as his successor. She took the throne in 1843 amid a serious struggle between conservative and liberal forces. She abdicated in 1868 under pressure from the military.

The Cortes chose Amadeus as her successor. His five-year rule was marked by bitter disputes. Amadeus abdicated in 1873. The Cortes established Spain's first republic. A military revolt ended the republic after a about a year. Alfonso XII, Isabella's son, was declared king. He was followed by Alfonso XIII in 1886. Many different radical and anarchist groups were gaining support across Spain during this time. Reform movements were violently opposed by landowners and their ally, the Catholic Church.

Independence moves were brutally suppressed in Cuba. Anti-Spanish guerrilla actions disturbed the United States, which feared the loss of American business investments. A United States Navy ship was sunk in Havana harbor with heavy loss of life in February of 1898.

American President McKinley ordered a blockade of Cuban ports in April of 1898, beginning the Spanish–American War. The United States Navy destroyed the Spanish naval fleet in Manila Bay in the Philippines the next month. American troops landed in Cuba and overcame the feeble Spanish opposition.

The 1899 Treaty of Paris all but ended Spain's empire. Cuba became independent. Puerto Rico, Guam and the Philippine Islands came under the control of the United States.

Spain remained neutral throughout World War I. The country experienced a much-needed economic boom. Left-wing elements gained strength in Spanish society. The Spanish Communist Party was formed in 1920. General Primo

Spain

de Rivera established a military dictatorship in 1923.

Victory by a republican majority in the 1931 elections prompted King Alfonso's abdication. The second Spanish Republic was established under President Alcalá Zamora. The vote was given to all adults and the power of the Catholic Church was restricted. Power passed to a center-right government after 1933.

The 1936 election produced a Popular Front government comprising socialists, communists and other groups. It was led by Manuel Azaña. This development provoked a civil war between the Nationalists and the Loyalists. The Nationalists were strongly unified under General Francisco Franco.

Nationalists captured much of northern Spain. Catalonia and the Basque region sided with the Loyalists against the Nationalists. The Nationalists had Madrid under siege by late 1936. Communist and socialist volunteers from across Europe formed International Brigades. They travelled to Spain to support the Loyalists.

The Nationalists received massive air force support from Germany. Italy sent 70,000 troops, calling them volunteers. Britain and France organized a non-intervention pact signed by twenty-seven nations. The Loyalists could rely on aid only from the Soviet Union. Their cause was not helped by a growing breach between communists and the other groups.

Nationalist forces had split the Loyalist army in half by late 1938. Catalonia fell to the Nationalists in January of 1939. They entered Madrid on April 1, 1939. The war had ended.

Franco moved quickly to consolidate control. He banned all political parties other than the Falangists, those who belonged to his Spanish Fascist Party. He made himself dictator of Spain. The Cortes was abolished and the autonomy of Catalan and Basque was terminated.

Spain did not participate in World War II, although it did support Germany and Italy. Franco was grateful for the aid they had supplied during the civil war. He was able to resist pressure from Germany's Adolf Hitler to enter the war. Franco began to liberalize his dictatorial policies as it became clear that the Allies were winning the war.

The United Nations refused to recognize the legitimacy of Franco's regime after the war. Spain eventually joined the organization in 1956. Many countries cut off diplomatic relations with Spain.

Spain struggled to integrate itself into the world economy during the 1950s. Labor relations were improved. Spain did not enjoy the same economic

Madrid's Palacio di Communicaciones

Spain is renowned for its beaches, such as this coastline at Sanfander.

development as other European countries during this time. Its strongest growth industry was tourism.

The last Spanish colonies, Morocco and Equatorial Guinea, gained their independence in the 1950s and 1960s. Spain had ample concerns within its own borders.

Political opposition to Franco was growing by the end of the 1950s. Industrial disputes had become everyday occurrences by the early 1960s. The Catholic Church, which had enjoyed enhanced power under Franco, began showing concerns about his methods. The Basque separatist movement, the ETA, was gaining strength. Franco instituted martial law in 1970, arresting ETA members and sentencing them to death. The government soon bowed to international pressure, lifted martial law and commuted its sentences against the ETA members. Nonetheless, the ETA assassinated Prime Minister Luis Carrero Blanco in 1973.

Constitutional changes opened up a quarter of the seats in the Cortes to direct election by the people in 1966. The government still exerted considerable influence on the media, although it had ended direct censorship. There was considerable expansion of secondary industry by the end of the 1960s.

Franco died on November 20, 1975, ending an era for Spain. King Juan Carlos ascended the throne of Spain, which was now a constitutional monarchy. The appointment of moderate Adolfo Suárez González as prime minister aided the king in proceeding with his plans for democratic reforms.

A new bicameral Cortes was inaugurated in 1977. The fascist Falange was dissolved and the Communist Party legalized. A new constitution was proclaimed the following year. Some autonomy was granted to the Basque country, Catalonia, and fifteen other regions in the late 1970s.

A group of military officers staged a coup in 1981. They seized the Cortes building. King Juan Carlos was able to convince the men to remain loyal to the government.

Vast amounts of foreign investment have flowed into Spain since the 1980s. New factories have been established and heavy industry is growing rapidly.

Basque separatists have continued their campaign of terrorism into the 2000s. Member of the al-Qaeda network were arrested in Spain after the September 11, 2001, attacks on the United States.

Sri Lanka

DEMOCRATIC SOCIALIST REPUBLIC OF SRI LANKA

Sri Lanka is an island in the Indian Ocean off the southeastern coast of India. The landscape is ruggedly beautiful, with coastal plains rising to plateaus. Mountains dominate the south central region. Some rivers and streams create rapids on the mountainsides, while others flow through deep valleys in the plateaus. Tropical rainforests covers half the island. The nation also includes a chain of tiny islands between its mainland and India. Sri Lanka's climate is equatorial, with high temperatures and humidity throughout the year. Heavy rainfall occurs between April and June and in October and November.

Three-quarters of the population is Sinhalese, twenty percent is Tamils. The rest are primarily Moors, with a Malay minority and a small community of Vedda people. Theravada Buddhism is the religion of the majority. Most of the Tamil people practice Hinduism. Sinhala and Tamil are the official languages.

Evidence of settlements dating back 12,000 years have been found on Sri Lanka. The tiny Vedda minority is most likely descended from that era. Their demise began with the arrival of the Sinhalese in the fifth century B.C.

The Sinhalese developed an agricultural society with an extensive irrigation system under King Vijaya. They established a capital at Anuradhapura and introduced Buddhism in the third century A.D. The realm was known as Sinhala.

Tamils crossed from southern India in the fourth century. They developed a strong base in the north. The Sinhalese were pushed into the southern regions. Native princes regained power in some areas during the twelfth and thirteenth centuries. Chinese forces occupied the island in the early fifteenth century.

Portuguese explorers arrived in 1517. They established friendly relations with native monarchs and founded a trading post at Colombo. The Portugese, who brought Catholicism to the island, soon came to control many areas. The Netherlands seized the island in 1658.

Britain expelled the Dutch in 1795, making it a crown colony three years later. Anti-colonial rebels in the Kandyan High-

The seated Buddha at Mihintale, where Buddhism originated in Sri Lanka.

LONELY PLANET IMAGES – CHRISTINE NIVEN

lands were finally suppressed in 1815. Ceylon, as it was then called, was devoted to the cultivation of tea, coffee and rubber.

Nationalists established the Ceylon National Congress soon after World War I. Great Britain drafted a new constitution for Ceylon, which provided indigenous people control over their national affairs.

The colony became an independent member of the Commonwealth of Nations on February 4, 1948. D. S. Senanayake was its first prime minister. The Colombo Plan was formulated in 1950. Commonwealth nations provided $340 million for economic development of the country under this program.

Sinhala became the national language in 1958. This prompted a wave of uprisings by Tamils. Sinhala supporters staged return attacks on Tamils.

Prime Minister S.W.R.D. Bandaranaike was assassinated by a Buddhist monk in 1959. His wife, Sirimavo, was elected prime minster the following year. She nationalized numerous foreign-owned businesses and banned the Tamil political party.

Relations with Britain and the United States improved in 1965 when the more moderate Dudley Senanayake regained the prime ministership.

Bandaranaike returned to power in 1970 as the economy continued to deteriorate. Her social security programs failed to please the communists, who attempted a coup in 1971. The rebellion was suppressed by police and military. The following year a new constitution changed the country to a republic. The name Ceylon was dropped in favor of Sri Lanka.

Repression of the Tamil language led to demands for a separate nation, called Eelam. The activities of the guerrilla group called Liberation Tigers of Tamil Eelam led to a state of emergency in 1983. President J. R. Jayawardene permitted 70,000 Indian troops to aid the Sri Lankan army in suppressing the Tamil Tigers in 1987.

President Ramasinghe Premadasa negotiated the withdrawal of Indian forces by March of 1990. He was assassinated by a suicide bomber in 1993. Government troops captured the Tamil stronghold of Jaffna. Tamil rebels staged suicide bombings and assassinations in Colombo. The war continued in other areas.

President Chandrika Kumaratunga was injured by a suicide bomber at an election rally in December 1999. A cease-fire was reached in February 2002. Further progress was made at secret peace talks held in Thailand during September 2002. The violence has virtually destroyed the country's once-lucrative tourist industry.

GOVERNMENT
Website www.priu.gov.lk
Capital Colombo
Type of government Republic
Independence from Britain
February 4, 1948 (dominion status)
Voting Universal adult suffrage
Head of state President
Head of government President
Constitution 1978
Legislature
Unicameral Parliament
Judiciary Supreme Court
Member of
CN, IMF, UN, UNESCO, WHO, WTO

LAND AND PEOPLE
Land area 25,332 sq mi
(65,620 sq km)
Highest point Pidurutalagala
8,281 ft (2,524 m)
Coastline 833 mi (1,340 km)
Population 19,408,635
Major cities and populations
Colombo 690,000
Dehiwala 205,000
Moratuwa 180,000
Ethnic groups Sinhalese 74%,
Tamil 18%, Moor 7%, Malay 1%
Religions Buddhism 69%,
Hinduism 15%, Christianity 8%,
Islam 8%
Languages Sinhala, Tamil (both
official), English

ECONOMIC
Currency Sri Lankan rupee
Industry
rubber processing, tea processing,
clothing, textiles, cement,
petroleum refining
Agriculture
rice, sugar cane, grains,
oilseed, spices, tea, rubber,
coconuts, dairy, beef
Natural resources
limestone, graphite, mineral sands,
gems, phosphates, clays

Sudan

REPUBLIC OF THE SUDAN

Located in northeastern Africa, Sudan is the largest country on that continent. The land rises sharply beyond the Red Sea coast. The barren Saharan plain covers the north one-third of the country. Central Sudan is made up of semi-arid steppes and low moutains. The south is a vast region of rain forests and swamps. The Blue Nile and White Nile rivers meet at Khartoum. The climate is tropical in the east, with some considerable heat and rainfall. Inland, there is little rainfall. Dust storms, called haboobs, are common in the desert areas.

Arabs and Nubians of the northern areas account for forty percent of the population. The central and southern peoples are mostly Nilotic and Sudanic Africans. Seventy percent of the population is Sunni Muslim. Arabic is the official language, although English is widely spoken. Indigenous languages are especially common in the south.

The northeast portion of Sudan was an ancient region known as Nubia at the time of Egyptian exploration in 2200 B.C. It was an Egyptian province by 1570 B.C. A Nubian revolt in the eighth century B.C. ended Egyptian control.

Coptic Christian kingdoms established in the sixth century A.D. endured for 800 years. The Muslim Funj overcame the Christians and held power until Egypt took control again in 1822.

British General Charles Gordon served as governor of Egyptian Sudan from 1877. He tried to suppress the slave trade. This provoked an uprising by fundamentalist Muslims known as the Mahdi. Gordon's forces were massacred in 1885 after a ten-month siege. British troops defeated the Mahdists in 1898.

Britain and Egypt controlled Sudan jointly for many difficult years. The Sudanese were gradually given self-government. Sudan became an independent republic on January 1, 1956.

The civilian government was overthrown in 1958 by General Ibrahim Abboud. Civilian government was restored in 1964, but overthrown by the military five years later. Political parties were banned and key industries nationalized.

President Nimeiry introduced Islamic law (Sharia) in 1983. This antagonized Christians. He was deposed two years later. Lieutenant-General Omar Ahmed al-Bashir's military regime suppressed all opposition in 1989. Bashir remains in power.

The United States attacked a suspected chemical weapons plant in August of 1998. Rampant human rights abuses continue to alarm international observers.

GOVERNMENT
Capital Khartoum
Type of government Republic
Independence from Britain
January 1, 1956
Voting Universal adult suffrage
Head of state President
Head of government President
Constitution 1973, partially suspended
Legislature
Unicameral National Assembly
Judiciary High Court
Member of IMF, OAU, UN, UNESCO, UNHCR, WHO

LAND AND PEOPLE
Land area 967,500 sq mi
(2,505,813 sq km)
Highest point Kinyeti
10,456 ft (3,187 m)
Coastline 530 mi (853 km)
Population 36,080,373
Major cities and populations
Khartoum 2,731,000
Omdurman 1,271,403
Port Sudan 320,000
Ethnic groups
African 52%, Arab 39%, others 9%
Religions Islam 75%, traditional animism 17%, Christianity 8%
Languages
Arabic (official), English, indigenous languages

ECONOMIC
Currency Sudanese dinar
Industry
oil, cotton processing, textiles, cement, edible oils, sugar milling, footwear, petroleum refining, pharmaceuticals, armaments, motor vehicles
Agriculture
cotton, nuts, sorghum, millet, wheat, gum arabic, sugar cane, tapioca, mangoes, papaya, bananas, sweet potatoes, sesame, livestock
Natural resources
petroleum, iron ore, copper, chromium, zinc, tungsten, mica, silver, gold

Suriname

REPUBLIC OF SURINAME

Suriname is located in northeastern South America. It has a wide, swampy coastal plain. The central plateau contains large tracts of grassland, dunes and some forests. Densely forested mountains cover much of the south. The climate is tropical. Heavy rains fall from April to August and November to February.

Thirty-five percent of Suriname's population is descended from African and indigenous people. A slightly smaller percentage are of Indian or Pakistani background. There are Javanese, Chinese and indigenous minorities. The main religions are Hinduism, Islam and Christianity. Dutch is the official language. Many people also speak Sranang Tongo, a dialect made from several languages.

Suriname was inhabited by the indigenous Arawak, Carib and Wattau peoples. The Dutch arrived in 1581. British traders began to colonize the area soon afterward. The Dutch West India Company imported slaves from Africa and established plantations in 1621.

Britain challenged Dutch control of the region. The Peace of Breda officially made Suriname a Dutch territory in 1667. Britain ceded their part of the area to the Netherlands in exchange for New Amsterdam (later New York City).

The Netherlands abolished slavery in 1863. Large numbers of laborers arrived from India and Java ten years later.

The colony had its own parliament from 1866. Netherlands Guiana became a full partner in the Kingdom of the Netherlands in 1954. The country, renamed Suriname, gained independence on November 25, 1975. Henck Arron was prime minister. Some 40,000 people chose to keep their Dutch citizenship by migrating to the Netherlands.

A military coup d'état installed Henk Chin A Sen as president on February 25, 1980. He was deposed by Sergeant-Major Désiré Bouterse, who suspended parliament and declared martial law.

Bloody clashes with the military peaked in late 1982. Guerrilla groups fought regular battles with government forces. They disrupted bauxite mining, which harmed the economy. Civilian government was restored in 1988, with Ramsewak Shankar as president. Bouterse ousted the civilian government in 1990.

The Suriname economy continued to decline through the 1990s. Bouterse was indicted by a Dutch court for drug trafficking in 1999. Ronald Venetiaan of the New Front coalition was elected president in 2000. The country is striving to find peace and democracy through the guidance of the Organization of American States (OAS).

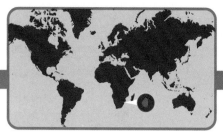

Swaziland

KINGDOM OF SWAZILAND

Landlocked Swaziland is in southeastern Africa. The eastern part of the country is a plateau. The Lebombo Moutains of the east give way to a central hilly grassland region. The mountains of the west reach heights of more than 4,000 feet (1,220 meters). Four main river systems flow west to east. The temperate climate features a rainy season from November to March.

All but three percent of the population is African. The remainder is European. The majority of the people are Chritians, but there is a significant number of people who practice animist religions. Both Siswati (Swazi) and English are official languages.

The original Bantu-speaking inhabitants of Swaziland arrived in the sixteenth century A.D., migrating from Mozambique. Swazi people, who settled between the Great Usutu and Pangola Rivers, were forced northward by Zulu attacks.

King Mswati asked for British protection from the Zulu in the 1850s. Europeans subsequently gained extensive land concessions. Britain made Swaziland a protectorate in 1894. Administration was transferred to Transvaal in the Union of South Africa (now the Republic of South Africa) nine years later.

Control tranferred to a British high commissioner in 1907.

Swaziland resisted South Africa's demands for incorporation into its territory in 1949. This decision was likely affected by South Africa's 1948, institution of apartheid.

Swaziland was granted limited self-government in 1963. It became fully independent on September 6, 1968 with King Sobhuza II as head of state. The king suspended the constitution in 1973 and banned all political activity. The 1978 constitution reinstated the parliament, but provided for almost absolute royal control.

The king died in 1982. His teenage son, Makhosetive, came to power. He was crowned King Mswati III in 1986, after a prolonged political struggle. Mswati dissolved parliament and announced he would rule by decree in 1992.

Harassment and persecution of pro-democracy activists was commonplace throughout the 1990s. Despite international pressure and trade union opposition, Mswati maintains absolute control. Suppression of political opposition continues.

The population of Swaziland has been seriously affected by Acquired Immune Deficiency Syndrome (AIDS). More than 25 percent of the adult population is infected with the virus that causes AIDS. Swaziland remains largely dependent upon economic aid from South Africa.

GOVERNMENT
Capital Mbabane
Type of government
Constitutional monarchy
Independence from Britain
September 6, 1968
Voting Universal adult suffrage
Head of state Monarch
Head of government Prime Minister
Constitution 1978
Legislature
Bicameral Parliament (Libandla)
House of Assembly (lower house),
Senate (upper house)
Judiciary High Court
Member of CN, IMF, OAU, UN, UNESCO, WHO, WTO

LAND AND PEOPLE
Land area 6,704 sq mi
(17,363 sq km)
Highest point Emlembe
6,109 ft (1,862 m)
Population 1,104,343
Major cities and populations
Mbabane 73,000
Ethnic groups
African 97%, European 3%
Religions
Christianity 70%, traditional animism 20%
Languages
Siswati, English (both official)

ECONOMIC
Currency Lilangeni
Industry
mining, wood pulp, sugar milling, beverages, textiles, apparel
Agriculture
sugar cane, cotton, corn, rice, citrus, pineapples, sorghum, peanuts, cattle, goats, sheep
Natural resources
asbestos, coal, clay, cassiterite, timber, quarry stone, talc

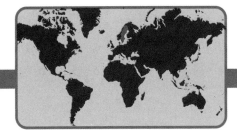

Sweden

KINGDOM OF SWEDEN

GOVERNMENT
Website www.sweden.gov.se
Capital Stockholm
Type of government
Constitutional monarchy
Voting Universal adult suffrage
Head of state Monarch
Head of government Prime
Minister
Constitution 1975
Legislature
Unicameral Parliament (Riksdag)
Judiciary Supreme Court
Member of CE, EU, IMF, OECD,
UN, UNESCO, UNHCR, WHO, WTO

LAND AND PEOPLE
Land area 173,732 sq mi
(449,964 sq km)
Highest point Mt. Kebnekaise
6,946 ft (2,117 m)
Coastline 2,000 mi (3,218 km)
Population 8,875,053
Major cities and populations
Stockholm 1,583,000
Göteborg 766,000
Malmö 255,000
Ethnic groups
Swedish 96%, Finnish 2%, others
2%
Religions Christianity
Languages
Swedish (official), Lapp, Finnish

ECONOMIC
Currency Swedish krona
Industry
iron, steel, precision bearings,
communications equipment,
armaments, aircraft, motor vehicles,
wood pulp, paper products,
processed foods
Agriculture
barley, wheat, beet sugar, meat,
dairy
Natural resources
zinc, iron ore, lead, copper,
silver, timber, uranium

Sweden occupies the eastern half of the Scandinavian peninsula in northwestern Europe. Thousands of lakes in the south central region make up just under ten percent of the country's total area. Fertile farmlands make up most of the remainder of central and southern Sweden. Sixty percent of the land is forested. The sparsely populated northern region is mountainous except for a narrow coastal strip. Sweden's climate features cold winters. Northern coastal waters are usually frozen in winter. Summers are mild.

The majority of Swedes live in urban areas. The population is almost completely of Swedish descent. About a half million people are Finnish, German, Norwegian, or Danish. The Lapps, who live in the far north, number close to 20,000.

Sweden is predominantly Christian. Ninety percent of the population claims membership in the Evangelical Lutheran Church. Most of the remainder espouse various other Protestant denominations.

The Swedish language is similar to Norwegian and Danish. It is derived from ancient Norse, with influences from German and English. Finnish and Lapp are commonly spoken in the north.

Sweden boasts a highly industrialized economy. It exports machinery, motor vehicles, electric and electronic equipment, steel, chemicals and textiles. Other major manufacturing industries include fine glassware, steel cutting instruments, refined petroleum and processed foods.

Agriculture is a small part of the economy, but it is scientifically advanced. Intensive fertilization and mechanization brings top returns from only seven percent of the country's land. Livestock and livestock products, including dairy items, are the primary farm commodities. Crops include barley, oats, potatoes, rye, sugar beets and wheat.

Flower stalls in Stockholm.

FLAT EARTH PICTURE GALLERY

Sweden

FLAT EARTH PICTURE GALLERY

Many other industries contribute to Sweden's thriving economy. Iron ore, lead, copper, and zinc are principal mined exports. Sweden is one of the largest suppliers of timber products in the world. Fishing is also significant. Tourism is a growing source of revenue for the country.

Sweden is a parliamentary democracy. The monarch is head of state, but real political power resides with the prime minister and cabinet. They are responsible to the unicameral parliament known as the Riksdag. Members of the Riksdag are elected by a vote of the people every three years. The 1975 constitution is a revision of the 1809 document.

The first known inhabitants of what is now Sweden appeared around 6000 B.C. The Svear people, who gave the country its name, developed a society about 2,000 years ago. They founded a kingdom in the region where Stockholm is today. They expanded their territory and fought regular wars with neighboring Götaland in the following centuries. The Svear defeated the Götar in the sixth century and consolidated control of much of southern Sweden.

Swedish warriors were part of the Viking forces that swept through much of Europe. Swedish adventurers also pushed eastwards into Russia, founding the settlement of Novgorod, and penetrated the southeast as far as Constantinople.

The Swedish kingdoms were constantly at war with Norway and Denmark. German and English missionaries, led by Anskar, introduced Christianity in the ninth century. King Eric invaded Finland in the mid-twelfth century, forcing Christianity upon the land. Finland came under Swedish control after about 200 years.

Sweden's metal fabricating industries rose to prominence in the fourteenth century, influenced by the Hanseatic League of German entrepreneurs. The growth of political power in the cities diminished the influence of the monarchs. The Union of Kalmar brought Sweden and Norway under the control of Denmark in 1397. Danish Queen Margaret I was unable to bring peace throughout the realm.

Rebellions led to the establishment of the Riksdag, Sweden's own parliament, during the fifteenth century. King Christian II massacred almost 100 Swedish nobles in an attempt to reassert Danish authority in 1520. This aggres-

Stockholm's Opera House

at Breitenfeld in 1631. Gustavus II was killed the following year at the Battle of Lutzen, but his influence remained. The 1648 Peace of Westphalia saw Sweden confirmed as a great European power.

King Charles X drove Denmark out of the southern part of the peninsula as well as the islands of Gotland and part of Norway in 1658. His heir, Charles XI, made himself absolute monarch in 1679, crippling the powers of the nobles.

Sweden was highly successful at the beginning of the Great Northern War (1700-1721). It invaded Russia in 1709

sion provoke a revolt which lead to independence for much of Sweden. The south remained under Danish control.

Gustav I was crowned Swedish king in 1523. He made Lutheranism the state religion, stripping the Catholic Church of its property. Although he was unable to regain southern Sweden, Gustav conquered Estonia in 1561.

Swedish King Johan III married the sister of the Polish king. Their son, Sigismund, became king of both countries in 1592. Sigismund was deposed in 1599 because of his Catholic faith.

The ascent of King Gustav II Adolph to the throne in 1611 launched a golden age of Swedish history. He defeated both

Russia and Poland and annexed large portions of their northwestern European territories.

He then intervened in the Thirty Years War on the Protestant side. Swedish forces invaded Germany, defeating those of the Habsburg Empire

Outdoor market stalls in Stockholm.

Sweden

only to be soundly defeated by the forces of Peter the Great. freedom of the press was introduced, and free trade encouraged. Sweden benefited greatly from the Industrial Revolution.

Relations with Norway were strained throughout the nineteenth century until the union was dissolved amicably in 1905. Sweden declared its neutrality in World War I. It entered into an agreement of mutual defense with Denmark and Norway. Sweden joined the League of Nations in 1920.

The government of Sweden again declared neutrality when World War II began. It made some concessions to Germany early on, then later aided the Allies. It maintained neutrality and saw its boundaries unchanged after the war.

Sweden became a model to the world in the decades following the war. Its ruling Social Democratic Party promoted economic growth and impressive expansion of social welfare programs. The nation pursued development of a vigorous program of international aid. A new constitution, adopted in 1975, dissolved the remaining power of the king.

The normally peaceful Swedish political scene was rocked by the assassination of Prime Minister Olaf Palme in 1986. Economic problems dominated the early 1990s. Austerity measures were introduced and numerous government enterprises were privatized. The economy improved by 2000.

Swedes were divided on the issue of membership of the European Union (EU). A 1994 vote narrowly confirmed approval for membership. Sweden officially joined the EU in January of 1995.

Stockholm's harbor and old town.

FLAT EARTH PICTURE GALLERY

Switzerland

SWISS CONFEDERATION

GOVERNMENT
Website www.admin.ch
Capital Bern
Type of government Republic
Voting Universal adult suffrage
Head of state President
Head of government President
Constitution 1874
Legislature
Bicameral Federal Assembly
National Council (lower house),
Council of States (upper house)
Judiciary Federal Supreme Court
Member of CE, IMF, OECD, UN,
UNESCO, UNHCR, WHO, WTO

LAND AND PEOPLE
Land area 15,491 sq mi
(41,299 sq km)
Highest point Dufourspitze
15,203 ft (4,634 m)
Population 7,283,274
Major cities and populations
Zurich 983,000
Bern 941,000
Geneva 450,000
Basel 410,000
Ethnic groups Swiss 60%, French
19%, Italian 4%, others 17%
Religions Christianity
Languages German, French,
Italian, Romansh (all official)

ECONOMIC
Currency Swiss franc
Industry machinery, chemicals,
watches, textiles, precision
instruments, pharmaceuticals,
tourism
Agriculture
grains, fruits, vegetables, meat, eggs
Natural resources
timber, salt

Switzerland is located in central Europe. More than half of its landscape is dominated by the Swiss Alps, which are part of the transcontinental range sweeping across numerous European countries. The Swiss landscape is rugged, with steep cliffs and deep valleys, threaded by rivers such as the Upper Rhine and the Rhône. The Swiss Plateau covers part of central Switzerland. This is the heart of the country's agricultural activities. Much of the population lives in this area. The Jura Mountains are found in the far northwest.

The Swiss climate varies greatly according to location and elevation. Switzerland's central plateau has cool winters and mild summers. Temperatures in the Alps fall well below freezing. Most of the landscape above 9,000 feet (2,743 meters) is covered with snow throughout the year.

Two-thirds of the population have a German-Swiss background, about twenty percent are French-Swiss and four percent are Italian-Swiss. Switzerland is overwhelmingly Christian. About 1.5 percent of the people follow Islam. There is also a small Jewish minority. Switzerland's four national languages are German, French, Italian and Romansh. Romansh is spoken by about one percent of population, primarily in the Graubunden region.

The Swiss economy revolves primarily around its role as a center of international trade and banking. Swiss banks are well known for their integrity and discretion.

The main agricultural activity is dairy farming. There is very little in the way of mining or mineral extraction. Precision machinery, timepieces, foods, textiles and wood products are exported to countries all over the world. Its pharmaceutical industry, based in Basel, is a world leader. Swiss handicrafts, such as music boxes, fine laces and wood carvings are widely prized.

**Colorful flowers frame
the elegant buildings
of Lausanne.**

FLAT EARTH PICTURE GALLERY

Switzerland

Unemployment in Switzerland is extremely low. The nation must rely on many guest workers from other countries. The Swiss enjoy one of the highest standards of living in the world. Their health care, general welfare and education standards are the highest of any European country.

Switzerland is a federation with a national government and a collection of states, known as cantons. It has a unique system of government based on the 1874 constitution, which has been amended many times since. There is a bicameral parliament known as the Federal Assembly. The upper house, called the Ständerat, is comprised of members from the various cantons, or states. The lower house, the Nationalrat, is elected for four years by a vote of the people.

Executive power lies with the seven-member Bundesrat, whose members are elected by the parliament. Each December the Ständesrat and the Nationalrat elect a new president and vice-president from the seven members of the Bundesrat. The constitution prohibits a president from serving two consecutive terms.

The original inhabitants of Switzerland were the Helvetii, who occupied the region between the Swiss Alps and the Jura Mountains. From them came Switzerland's alternative name, Helvetia, which is used on its postage stamps.

The Helvetii prospered greatly as part of the Roman Empire from the first century B.C. to the fifth century A.D. Germanic tribes called the Burgundii and Alemanni invaded in the fifth century. These tribes were conquered by the Frankish Empire in the next century. It was split between the duchy of Swabia and the kingdom of Burgundy in the ninth century.

Reunification came as part of the Holy Roman Empire under Conrad II in 1033. It consisted of a number of city-states which later became cantons.

Holy Roman Emperor Rudolf, of the powerful Austrian Habsburg dynasty, tried to exert tighter control over the Swiss. Many people saw this as a threat to their individual liverties. Three cantons called Uri, Unterwalden and Schwyz formed the Perpetual League to resist control by the Austrian Habsburgs. This is considered to be the birth of the Swiss Federation. The Habsburgs were defeated at Morgarten in 1315, prompting five more cantons to join the league. Together they inflicted severe defeats on the Habsburgs at Sempach in 1386 and Näfels in 1388.

Holy Roman Emperor Maximiliani was defeated in a last attempt to subdue the Swiss in 1499. The resulting Treaty of Basel recognized the virtual independence of the Swiss. Defeat at the hands of France in 1515 prompted the confeder-

Regions such as Spiez are typical of the Swiss landscape.

Trams and pedestrians share the streets of Bern, the capital of Switzerland

FLAT EARTH PICTURE GALLERY

ation to adopt a policy of neutrality which persists to this day.

Further conflict resulted from the Reformation which swept into Switzerland from Germany in the early sixteenth century. It pitted Calvinists against Catholics across the country. Switzerland did not participate in the Thirty Years War fought between Catholics and Protestants from 1618. It did benefit, however, when its independence was confirmed by the 1648 Peace of Westphalia.

Switzerland grew wealthy in the following years. It was dominated by intellectual and artistic pursuits. The canton governments gradually fell into the hands of a small, conservative, wealthy elite.

French armies invaded Switzerland and established the Helvetic Republic in 1798, following the French Revolution. The new centralized government broke the power of the cantons. This situation lasted until Napoleon restored some powers to the cantons in 1803. The Congress of Vienna reaffirmed Switzerland's neutrality and the old order was restored at the end of the Napoleonic

Wars. The desire for a more representative democracy provoked a minor war between the conservative Catholic cantons and the rest of the country in 1847.

The constitution of 1848 established the federal structure. It featured a central government and parliament, while the cantons retained certain specific powers. A new constitution, adopted in 1874, formally granted the people the right to influence legislation through intiative and referendum.

Switzerland maintained its neutrality through World Wars I and II. Both wars brought costly economic depression. The German, French and Italian Swiss stood firm against the threat of invasion.

Switzerland joined the League of Nations in 1920. The league established its headquarters at Geneva. Switzerland decided against joining the United Nations after World War II. It feared that membership would jeopardize its policy of neutrality. Switzerland finally voted for membership in a 2002 referendum.

Switzerland became a member of the International Monetary Fund in 1992. It has been a member of the European Free Trade Association since 1972, but it has not joined the European Union.

Women were given the right to vote in federal elections and hold federal office in 1971. More than ten percent of the seats in the Nationalrat were held by women as of 1979. Switzerland's first woman president, Ruth Dreifuss, served in 1999.

In March of 1997, the Swiss government announced plans to establish a $4.7 billion fund to aid Holocaust survivors and victims of catastrophes. The announcement came in response to pressure from Jewish groups and others who claimed that authorities in Switzerland had failed to return assets seized by Nazis and deposited in Swiss banks during World War II.

Syria

SYRIAN ARAB REPUBLIC

Located in southwestern Asia, Syria has a coastline on the Mediterranean Sea. A narrow coastal plain extends in from the Mediterranean. The Jabal an-Nusayriyah moutain range lies parallel to this plain. The Anti-Lebanon range in the south tapers off to the Golan Heights, a hilly region in the southwest. The landscape eventually gives way to the Syrian Desert in the southeast. Much of the rest of the country is a plateau bisected by the valley of the Euphrates River.

The climate on the Mediterranean coast features warm, dry summers and mild winters. Rainfall is heaviest in mountain areas. The desert is dry, with very high temperatures. The hot, dry Khamsin wind blows across the desert from the east.

Almost all Syrians are of Arab descent. Three-quarters of the population is Sunni Muslim. Other Muslim sects include the Alawites, Ismailis and Shi'ites. Greek and Armenian Orthodox Christians make up about ten percent. Religious minorities also include Druses, who follow a religion related to Islam. There is a tiny Jewish community. Arabic is the official language.

Syria has a large agricultural sector concentrated in western

The spectacular Umayyad Mosque at Damascus.

coastal regions. There is an extensive irrigation system. The main crops are wheat, beet sugar, barley, potatoes, cotton and lentils. The main secondary industries are oil refining, chemicals, textiles and processed foods. Pipelines from Iraq bring oil to Syria's ports.

Most industry in Syria was nationalized prior to the early 1960s. Considerable privatization has occurred since that time.

The president is elected by the people for a seven-year term. Government ministers, including the prime minister and three vice-presidents, are appointed by the president. Members of the legislature, the People's Council, are popularly elected to four-year terms.

Northeastern Syria was inhabited as far back as 4000 BC. King Shamshi-Adad is of Assyria is thought to have established his capital, Shubat Enlil, in northeast Syria, in 1800 B.C. The kingdom was later conquered by Hammurabi of Babylonia. Parts of the region were later conquered by Egyptians, Hittites and Assyrians.

Persia became dominant in the sixth century B.C., remaining until Alexander the Great's conquest in 333 B.C. Seleucid, one of Alexander's generals, took control about 300 B.C. During the next centuries, the Seleucids and Egyptians fought for possession of lower Syria

and Palestine. Both areas, as well as much of western Asia, passed to the Seleucids, whose kingdom became known as Syria.

Syria was made a Roman province in A.D. 64. Christianity was introduced at this time. It become part of Byzantium after the Roman Empire's collapse in the fourth century.

The spread of Christianity was stifled by a Muslim Arab invasion. Damascus became the capital of the Umayyad caliphate in 661. The Umayyad dynasty spread itself west across northern Africa, into southern Spain, and east into India. The Abbasids conquered the Umayyads in 750.

The Christian crusaders from Europe attempted to drive Muslims out of the Holy Land, which included Syria, beginning in the eleventh century. Christians and Muslims had coexisted peacefully in Syria before this time. The Crusaders incorporated part of the region into the Christian kingdom of Jerusalem. Some of the area became part of the principality of Antioch. The Seljuk Turks, led by the great Saladin, drove the crusaders out in the late twelfth century.

Mongols laid waste to much of Syria in 1260. They were finally expelled by Egyptians who controlled Syria until 1516. The Turkish Ottoman Empire took control at that time. They

GOVERNMENT
Capital Damascus
Type of government Republic
Independence from France (UN Trust Territory)
April 17, 1946
Voting Universal adult suffrage
Head of state President
Head of government Prime Minister
Constitution 1973
Legislature
Unicameral People's Council
Judiciary
Supreme Constitutional Court
Member of
AL, IMF, OECD, UN, UNESCO, WHO

LAND AND PEOPLE
Land area 71.500 sq mi
(185,180 sq km)
Highest point
Mount Hermon
9,232 ft (2,814 m)
Coastline 120 mi (193 km)
Population 16,728,808
Major cities and populations
Damascus 2.3 million
Aleppo 2.1 million
Homs 655,000
Ethnic groups
Arab 90%, Kurd 7%, others 3%
Religions
Muslim 90%, Christian 9%, others 1%
Languages Arabic (official)

ECONOMIC
Currency Syrian pound
Industry
petroleum, textiles, food processing, beverages, mining
Agriculture
wheat, barley, cotton, lentils, chickpeas, olives, beef, mutton, eggs, poultry, dairy
Natural resources
petroleum, phosphates, chrome, manganese, asphalt, iron ore, rock salt, marble, gypsum

Syria

maintained power for the next four centuries.

Strong nationalist movements began in the early 1900s. Britain encouraged Syrians to join the Allied Powers in opposing Turkey during World War I. Britain guaranteed independence for Syria at the end of the war. European powers arranged for a League of Nations mandate that placed Syria under French control in 1920. Independence did not come at this time.

The people of Syria strongly resented the French presence. They staged armed rebellions, strikes and riots during the 1920s. French and Syrian leaders wrote a treaty for substantial Syrian independence in 1938, but France never signed the document. France ceded the district of Alexandretta to Turkey the following year. The ancient Syrian capital of Antioch was located in this area.

The French administration of Syria declared loyalty to the pro-Nazi Vichy regime during World War II. British and Free French forces invaded, securing the territory for the Allies in June 1941. France established a Syrian republic. Shukri al-Kuwatli became president in the elections of 1943. French troops left the country on April 17, 1946, the date Syria recognizes as its independence day.

Syria participated in the unsuccessful 1948 war between Arab forces and the newly established state of Israel. Three military coups occurred in 1949. The last was engineered by Lieutenant-Colonel Adib al-Shishakli. A new constitution was introduced in 1950 and Hashim al-Atasi was elected president.

Shishakli led another coup which forced Atasi's resignation in 1951. He and his associates formed a new government and adopted a new constitution in 1953. Shishakli ruled as a dictator, severely severely curbing civil liberties. A coup the next year restored Atasi to the presidency and reinstated the 1950 constitution.

Syria and Egypt formed the United Arab Republic (UAR) in February 1958. Gamal Abdel Nasser of Egypt became president of the federation. He dissolved all Syrian political parties, including the Communist party, and dismissed pro-Soviet army officers. The rapid nationalization of industries and land reform intensified opposition to the UAR. Syria withdrew from the UAR in 1961.

Several former political parties merged to form the Ba'ath Party. It became the dominant power in Syrian politics, with pro-Arab and socialist policies.

A dispute with Israel over the waters of the Jordan River was a factor in the Six-Day War in 1967. Israel captured Syria's Golan Heights and retained it after the conflict.

General Hafiz al-Assad seized power in 1970. He became president the following year. More than half of government posts were filled by Ba'ath party members.

The 1973 Yom Kippur War saw Israel and Syria once again battling for control of the Golan Heights. Israel withdrew to its previous position after a cease-fire agreement was signed in 1974. A United Nations buffer zone was established between the two nations.

The radical Muslim Brotherhood staged an uprising in Hamah in 1982. Thousands died before it was ended by government troops. The Soviet Union's collapse in the late 1980s prompted moves to improve relations with western Europe and the United States. Syria condemned Iraq's invasion of Kuwait in 1990. Its troops joined coalition forces.

Peace talks with Israel continued, but Syria's demand for Israel's withdrawal from the Golan Heights remained an obstacle. Negotiations began again when a new Israeli government was elected in 1999.

President Assad died in 2000. His son Bashar al-Assad became president and leader of both the army and the Ba'ath Party. Some economic and social liberalization has occurred since that time.

Taiwan

REPUBLIC OF CHINA

Formerly known as Formosa, Taiwan is made up of one large island and several smaller islands off the southeastern coast of China. It is surrounded by the East China Sea, the Pacific Ocean and the South China Sea. The eastern side of the main island is dominated by mountains running from north to south. The western region is a broad, fertile coastal plain which receives substantial rainfall.

The tropical monsoon has a major effect on Taiwan. Summers are hot and humid, winters are cool. The higher regions are cooler. Summer typhoons (hurricanes) sweep in from the ocean regularly. Most rain falls during summer.

A large proportion of Taiwan's people are descended from Han Chinese, who arrived in 1949 following the communist takeover of their homeland. Around two percent of the population are aboriginal people, of Malay background. Most of these people live in the mountains.

About half of Taiwan's people espouse either Buddhism or Taoism. There is also a strong Christian community. A large remainder of people acknowledge no religious affiliation. Mandarin is the official language, but various other Chinese dialects, such as Fukienese, are also spoken. The traditional Mandarin script is the basis of the written language.

Taiwan, as one of Asia's leading trading countries, is also one of its wealthiest. It avoided the disastrous Asian economic downturn in 1997–98. Taiwan specializes in computers, electronic equipment, motor vehicles, chemicals, machinery, ships and steel. Only the United States and Japan have larger computer hardware industries.

Taiwan's government is complex. When the Nationalists fled mainland China in 1949, they set up a government-in-exile in Taiwan. This government was

Part of the skyline of Taipei, Taiwan's capital city.

SCOTT BRODIE

Taiwan

considered to be the official ruling body of all China. This belief remains largely unchanged today, although it is not recognized by most of the rest of the world.

Thus, there is a government of the Republic of China, as Taiwan is officially known, and a separate government for the province of Taiwan. The president of the republic is elected by the people for a six-year term. The president appoints a cabinet and prime minister. The parliament is known as the Legislative Yuan. Its 334 members are elected to four-year terms.

The original Taiwanese were Malay aborigines. The first Chinese arrived in the seventh century A.D. from China's Fujian and Guangdong provinces. Bands of Japanese are said to have conquered portions of the islands in the twelfth century.

Portuguese explorers named the island Formosa, meaning beautiful, in 1590. The Netherlands established a base in the south during 1624, near present-day Tainan. The Spanish did the same in the north. They were expelled by the Dutch in 1641. A Ming dynasty general, fleeing China's new Manchu rulers, established a kingdom on Taiwan in 1662. This kingdom lasted until the Manchus made it part of the Chinese Empire near the end of the century.

Buildings covered with advertising in Taipei's shopping district.

SCOTT BRODIE

The Treaty of Tientsin (Tianjin) ended a victorious British and French War against China in 1858. Two ports on the eastern coast of Taiwan were opened to foreign ships. Christian missionaries from Europe arrived soon afterward.

China ceded Formosa to Japan at the end of the Sino-Japanese War in 1895. Large-scale industrialization and railway construction was commenced by the Japanese. Chinese rebellions were put down. Japanese culture was rigidly imposed.

Formosa was returned to Chinese control when Japan was defeated at the end of World War II. A Taiwanese revolt against Chinese authorities was brutally suppressed. Taiwan was proclaimed a province of China.

General Chiang Kai-shek's Nationalist was government of China was gradually defeated by Communist armies between 1945 and 1949. The Nationalists fled to Taiwan.

Chiang Kai-shek established the Republic of China with its headquarters at Taipei. A Chinese invasion in 1950 was prevented by the United States Navy's Seventh Fleet.

The United States extended considerable economic and military aid to Taiwan. It fervently supported Taiwan as the rightful government of China. Most other countries recognized the communist People's Republic of China (PRC) of Beijing. The United States maintained substantial military bases in Taiwan.

Land reform was introduced. Large estates were broken up and handed over to former peasants. The industrial structure established by Japan was hugely expanded in the 1950s. This was greatly assisted by United States aid, which ended in 1965, having become unnecessary. A total of $4 billion had flowed from the U.S. into Taiwan's economy by that time.

Taiwan retained the China seat in the United Nations General Assembly and its place on the Security Council. This remained the case until 1971. A U.N. resolution replaced the Republic of China with the PRC.

U.S. President Richard Nixon visited China in 1972, marking a thawing in the previously frosty relations between Beijing and Washington. A reduction of United States forces on Taiwan began. The United States officially recognized the PRC as the official China in 1979. It did retain its defense commitment to Taiwan.

Chiang Kai-shek died in 1975, during his sixth term as president. His son, Chiang Ching-kuo, began a process of liberalization. The country developed a dynamic, free-enterprise culture. Improved relations with the PRC enabled Taiwan's people to visit the mainland beginning in 1987.

Martial law was finally lifted in 1987. Political prisoners were released and political parties were legalized in 1989. Lee Teng-hui, elected president in 1988, reformed the Legislative Yuan. Many delegates were those elected on the mainland in 1947.

The Democratic Progressive Party (DPP) gained popularity in the 1990s. It proposed Taiwan drop its pretense of being the government of China and become an independent nation. China fired tests missiles near the coast of Taiwan soon after the elections were held. Many believed that this was a demonstration of its territorial claim to Taiwan.

The pro-independence President Lee was re-elected by a huge majority, indicating the feelings of the people. The DPP's Chen Shui-bian was elected president in 2000.

The rising cost of labor affected Taiwan's manufacturing industries during the 1990s. Some large corporations began establishing factories in southern China where labor is less expensive. Taiwan began evolving into a research and design center for high-technology products.

Today, Taiwan is officially recognized by only a small number of countries. Many nations wish to retain contact because of its economic power. Taiwan's foreign relations are more or less handled by the business sector. They conduct the diplomacy normally carried out by embassies and consulates.

The concept of Taiwan as an independent nation is strongly supported by about eighty percent of the population. President Chen, who refers to China and Taiwan as "different countries," is supportive of a referendum on formal independence.

Motor scooters are the most popular form of personal transport in Taiwan.

Tajikistan

REPUBLIC OF TAJIKISTAN

Tajikistan, in central Asia, is a member of the Commonwealth of Independent States (CIS). The terrain of Tajikistan is extremely mountainous. The Pamir Moutains and the high Pamir Plateau make up much of the eastern part of the country. Large glaciers feed numerous swift-flowing streams which provide great potential for generating hydroelectric power. Earthquakes are commonplace. Winter temperatures are extremely low in the mountains. Summers in the valleys can be very warm.

Sixty-five percent of the people are ethnic Tajik. Twenty-five percent are Uzbeks, and there are Russian, Tatar, Kyrgyz and Ukrainian minorities. Eighty percent are Sunni Muslims. A very small minority is Christian. About twelve percent acknowledge no religion. Tajik is the official language, but Russian is widely spoken.

Migrants from Iran arrived in the area of Tajikistan during ancient times. It was part of the Persian Empire until conquered by Alexander the Great in the fourth century B.C. Arab conquers of the seventh and eighth centuries A.D. introduced Islam. Mongols invaded in the thirteenth century A.D. Tajikistan was incorporated into the Khanate of Bukhara in the 1500s. It became a Russian protectorate in the 1880s.

Bukhara rebelled against Russian rule at the end of the Russian Revolution in 1917. It held out against the Russian army until 1921. It was then made an autonomous republic within the Uzbek Soviet Socialist Republic. Uzbeck became a part of the Union of Soviet Socialist Republics (USSR) in 1924.

The republic became known once again as Tajikistan when it declared its independence from the USSR in September of 1991. It joined the CIS later that year. A bloody civil war ensued. Some 60,000 people were killed, 600,000 were displaced and 300,000 fled the country. Communists, supported by Russian troops, controlled the government for a time in the mid-1990s. Anti-government guerillas were operating from Afghanistan.

Voters approved a new constitution in 1994. Imomali Rakhmonov was elected president. He survived a suicide attempt in 1997. An agreement for resolving differences with rebel leaders and establishing a viable multiparty coalition government was signed shortly thereafter. International observers have noted numerous irregularities in recent presidential and parliamentary elections. The People's Democratic Party firmly dominates.

GOVERNMENT
Capital Dushanbe
Type of government Republic
Independence from Soviet Union
September 9, 1991
Voting Universal adult suffrage
Head of state President
Head of government Prime Minister
Constitution 1994
Legislature
Bicameral Supreme Assembly
Assembly of Representatives
(lower house), National Assembly
(upper house)
Judiciary Supreme Court
Member of
IMF, UN, UNESCO, WHO

LAND AND PEOPLE
Land area 55,250 sq mi
(143,100 sq km)
Highest point
Communism Peak
24,599 ft (7,498 m)
Population 6,578,681
Major cities and populations
Dushanbe 600,000
Kujand 190,000
Ethnic groups
Tajik 65%, Uzbek 25%, others 10%
Religions
Islam 85%, Christian 2%
Languages Tajik (official), Russian

ECONOMIC
Currency Somoni
Industry
aluminum, mining, chemicals,
fertilizers, cement, vegetable oil,
machine tools, electrical appliances
Agriculture
cotton, grain, fruits, grapes,
vegetables, cattle, sheep, goats
Natural resources
petroleum, uranium, mercury,
brown coal, lead, zinc, antimony,
tungsten, silver, gold

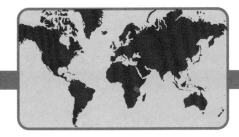

Tanzania

UNITED REPUBLIC OF TANZANIA

GOVERNMENT
Website www.tanzania.go.tz
Capital Dar es-Salaam
Type of government Republic
Independence from Britain
Zanzibar December 19, 1963
Tanganyika April 26,1961
Voting Universal adult suffrage
Head of state President
Head of government President
Constitution 1977
Legislature
Unicameral National Assembly
Judiciary High Court
Member of CN, IMF, OAU, UN,
UNESCO, UNHCR, WHO, WTO

LAND AND PEOPLE
Land area 364,879 sq mi
(945,037 sq km)
Highest point Kilimanjaro
19,340 ft (5,895 m)
Coastline
885 mi (1,424 km)
Population 36,232,074
Major cities and populations
Dar es-Salaam 2.3 million
Mwanza 260,000
Dodoma 210,000
Ethnic groups
Bantu 99%, others 1%
Religions
Christianity 45%,
Islam 35%, traditional animism 20%
Languages
Swahili, English (both official),
indigenous languages

ECONOMIC
Currency Tanzanian shilling
Industry
beverages, sugar milling, sisal
twine, mining, oil refining,
footwear, cement, textiles, wood
products, fertilizer, salt
Agriculture
coffee, sisal, tea, cotton, pyrethrum
nuts, cloves, corn, wheat, tapioca,
bananas, fruits, vegetables, livestock
Natural resources
tin, phosphates, iron ore, coal,
diamonds, gemstones, gold,
natural gas, nickel

Tanzania, on central Africa's eastern coast, includes the mainland area as well as the islands of Zanzibar and Pemba in the Indian Ocean. Much of the coastal mainland is swampy and low-lying. The inland is predominantly plateau. The volcanic Mount Kilimanjaro, near Tanzania's northeast border, is Africa's highest point. Lakes Nyasa and Tanganyika lie in the Great Rift Valley, which crosses the country from north to south. The island of Zanzibar is the largest coral island near Africa. The coastal climate is equatorial, the inland is more temperate.

Most of the population is made up of various Bantu-speaking peoples. The largest group is the Sukuma. Other major groups include the Nyawezi, Haya and Swahili. Nearly half of the population is Christian, while a third are Muslim. Swahili and English are the official languages.

Tanzania was made up of Tanganyika and Zanzibar prior to 1964. Human habitation of Tanganyika has been traced back 1.75 million years. Bantu-speaking peoples arrived in the sixth century A.D. Germany annexed the inland regions in 1884. The German East Africa Company allocated land to German settlers, antagonizing indigenous peoples.

The country came under the control of Britain by a League of Nations mandate in 1918. During the next several decades the country faired better than many others in terms of race relations. The Tanganyika African National Union led the way to independence in 1961. Julius Nyerere was elected president.

Arabs established trading posts on Zanzibar as early as the eighth century. Explorer Vasco da Gama landed in 1498. Portugese traders displaced the Arabs. In 1587, the Zimba people massacred 3,000 people at Kilwa. Portugal was replaced by Oman from the mid-eighteenth century. Zanzibar was declared a British protectorate in 1890.

Zanzibar became independent in December of 1963. Its sultan was deposed and a republic created in early 1964. President Nyerere of Tanganyika and Prime Minister Karume of Zanzibar began talks which led to the formation of Tanzania in April of 1964. A one-party state was declared and key industries nationalized. Tanzania actively opposed apartheid in South Africa and Idi Amin's regime in Uganda.

Ali Hassan Mwinyi replaced Nyerere as president in 1985. The nation began liberalizing its economy. The United States blamed an international terrorist network for a bomb blast which killed 11 and injured 70 near the American embassy in Dar es-Salaam in 1998.

Thailand

KINGDOM OF THAILAND

Thailand is a kingdom in Southeast Asia. It lies within the Indochinese Peninsula, except for a southernmost strip which occupies the Malay Peninsula. Thailand faces the Gulf of Thailand on the southeast and the Andaman Sea on the southwest. Mountain systems dominate the terrain throughout much of the country. Mountain ranges run from north to south in the northern and western areas. The northeast is a semi-arid plateau region best suited to grazing animals. Much of central Thailand is a flat, highly fertile region near the Chao Praya River. The climate is tropical, with heavy rainfall and intense humidity.

Seventy-five percent of the people are ethnic Thais. About fifteen percent are Chinese. There are also Mon and Khmer minorities. Indigenous groups include the Lana, Semang, Karen and Chao Nam.

All but five percent of the population is Theravada Buddhist. Most of the remainder are Muslims. Thai is the official language.

More than half the population is involved in agricultural production, mostly on small farms. Thailand is a major exporter of rice. It also exports rubber, sugar and corn.

Manufacturing has traditionally centered on footwear, clothing and associated products. The development of high-technology production has enabled Thailand to become a major manufacturer of electronic equipment, computer components and domestic appliances.

Thailand is one of the world's most popular tourist destinations. The relaxed Thai lifestyle and unique culture attracts people from all over the world. Thailand also boasts one of the most appealing environments in Asia.

Thailand is a constitutional monarchy. The hereditary monarch is head of state and commander of the armed forces. The monarch appoints the cabinet and prime minister.

The prime minister must be an elected member of the National Assembly. The National Assembly is a bicameral parliament. The people elect members of the House of Representatives for four-years and members of the Senate for six years.

Archaeological discoveries indicate a primitive cave-dwelling culture existed 10,000 years ago. Tai-speaking people moved into the area from China in the second century B.C. Tai leaders developed the kingdom of Nan Chao about A.D. 220. They were constantly under threat of invasion by the Khmers to the east. Various chieftains united to provide defense against the Khmer. They created the independent Sukhothai kingdom was established in 1238.

Most prominent of the Sukhothai kings was Ramkamhaeng, crowned in 1279. He introduced Theravada Buddhism and developed the writing system that is the basis of today's Thai script. He also expanded the kingdom considerably.

The Ayutthaya kingdom was on the rise by the fourteenth century. Under King Borom Rachathirat, it absorbed Sukhothai in 1378. Ayutthaya kings took the title of Devaraja, or God King. Ayutthaya conquered the great Khmer center of Angkor in 1431.

FLAT EARTH PICTURE GALLERY

The elephant is greatly revered in Thai culture.

Spain, the Netherlands and Britain all established trading posts in Thailand around 1600. Japanese military experts commanded the bodyguards for King Song Tham from 1610 to 1628. Catholic missionaries arrived from France in 1662.

The Burmese Empire again conquered Ayutthaya in 1767. They seized vast amounts of gold and other goods. Ayutthayan General Phya Taksin assembled a formidable army and navy in the south and expelled the invaders. Taksin was proclaimed king. He moved the capital to Thonburi, near today's Bangkok. Laos and Cambodia became part of the kingdom.

Taksin died in 1782. He was replaced by General Chakri, who was crowned Rama I. He founded the dynasty from which the present king is descended. He moved the capital to Bangkok and built the Temple of the Emerald Buddha and the Grand Palace. The kingdom became known as Siam.

Legal experts revamped the nation's laws. Various Buddhist practices were adapted to Siamese culture. Areas of lower Burma, Chiang Mai in the north, and the Malay states of Kedah, Perlis, Kelantan and Trengganu, were annexed during Rama I's reign.

The Portuguese arrived in 1511, agreeing to aid the kingdom in its wars in return for trading rights. Ayutthaya repelled Burmese invasions with Portugese assistance until 1569, when Burma finally prevailed. Most Ayutthayan people were forcibly removed to Burma.

Fifteen-year-old Prince Naresuen assembled a guerrilla army and freed Ayutthaya in 1584. He ascended to the throne in 1590 as Naresuen the Great. Ayutthaya grew and prospered for two hundred years. It became a great city.

GOVERNMENT
Website www.thaigov.go.th
Capital Bangkok
Type of government
Constitutional monarchy
Voting
Universal compulsory adult suffrage
Head of state
British Crown,
represented by Governor-General
Head of government Prime Minister
Constitution 1997
Legislature
Bicameral Parliament (Rathasapha)
House of Representatives (lower house), Senate (upper house)
Judiciary Supreme Court
Member of APEC, ASEAN, IMF, OECD, UN, UNESCO, UNHCR, WHO, WTO

LAND AND PEOPLE
Land area 198,115 sq mi (513,115 sq km)
Highest point Doi Inthanon 8,451 ft (2,576 m)
Coastline 2,000 mi (3,219 km)
Population 61,797,751
Major cities and populations
Bangkok 7.3 million
Nonthaburi 280,000
Ethnic groups
Thai 75%, Chinese 15%, others 10%
Religions Buddhism 95%, Islam 4%
Languages
Thai (official), indigenous languages

ECONOMIC
Currency Baht
Industry
textiles,, jewelry, electric appliances, computers, furniture, plastics, mining
Agriculture
rice, tapioca, rubber, corn, sugar cane, coconuts, soybeans
Natural resources
tin, rubber, natural gas, tungsten, tantalum, timber, lead, fluorite, gypsum, lignite, seafood

Thailand

SCOTT BRODIE

Rama IV, also known as King Mongkut, opened up international trade and built roads and canals. He imported foreign advisers to upgrade government offices and the army and to organize a police force. King Chulalongkorn (Rama V), who reigned from 1868 to 1910, made history when he travelled to Europe in 1897.

Siam fought alongside the Allies in World War I. It was a founding member of the League of Nations.

Siam's rice export markets collapsed during the Depression. King Prajadhipok (Rama VII) ordered severe

One of the buildings in the Royal Palace grounds, Bangkok.

budget cuts for the civil service and military. This provoked a revolt against the government in 1932, led by Dr. Pridi Phanomyong. Civilian and military leaders forced the King to accept a new constitution ending his absolute powers.

Another coup d'état in June of 1933 deposed Prime Minister Manopakorn. Colonel Phanon Phomphayuhasena took his place. Opposition to Phanon's policies resulted in a third coup in October of 1933. The insurgents demanded a return to the absolute monarchy. This time the coup was put down in six days.

The King fled Siam for Europe in 1934. Phanon held power until 1939, when he was replaced by Phibun Songgram. Phibun changed Siam's name to Thailand (Land of the Free). Phibun's government made demands on France beginning in 1940. It sought the return of lands ceded to France decades earlier. Thailand received parts of present-day Cambodia and Laos.

Thailand allied itself with Japan during World War II. It declared war on the United

States and Britain. The Free Thai movement was established by Dr. Pridi Phanomyong, who had inspired the 1932 revolution. The movement secretly collaborated with the Allies during the war.

Phibun's government was overthrown in 1944. The Thai people united under Pridi and developed sincere ties with the Allied powers.

Thailand signed a treaty with Great Britain and India in 1946. It renounced its claims to Malayan territory gained during the war. Relations with the U.S. resumed and Thailand joined the United Nations.

King Ananda Mahidol died under suspicious circumstances in 1946. His brother, Bhumibol

SCOTT BRODIE

A royal statue contrasts with a modern office block in Bangkok.

Adulyedej, became prince regent for four years before being crowned King Rama IX.

Fears of a communist invasion prompted a military *coup d'état* in 1947. Phibun was restored as prime minister. He ruled as a dictator, while working to maintain strong relations with the U.S. and Great Britain. Phibun was overthrown in another coup. Field Marshal Sarit Thanarat appointed Thanom Kittikachorn prime minister. A year later, Sarit removed Thanom and declared himself prime minister. Thailand came under martial law.

Sarit governed in a harsh authoritarian style for five years. He concentrated on economic growth and attracting foreign investors. Sarit died in 1963, Thanom Kittikachorn returned to the leadership. American military bases were established in Thailand to support the growing war in Vietnam. Large numbers of Thai soldiers served in Vietnam.

The 1968 constitution revived civilian rule, with Thanom Kittikachorn as prime minister. Worsening economic conditions led, in 1971, to yet another military *coup d'état*. The economy revived in 1972, aided by an influx of many U.S. military personnel who had left Vietnam.

The 1970s through the 1980s was a time of great instablity for Thailand's government. Dis-

A fish vendor's stall in the Lampang marketplace.

FLAT EARTH PICTURE GALLERY

content among Thai people led to a week of rioting by students in Bangkok in 1973. Thanom was forced to resign. Three different constitutions were adopted between 1972 and 1978. Short-lived civilian governments were followed by military coups and violence. Although Thailand prospered in the 1980s, Thais were far from happy with their lack of dem ocracy.

Another new constitution was adopted in 1991. Pro-military parties won the elections in March of 1992. Hundreds of thousands of people demonstrated in protest. Police killed more than 100 demonstrators and arrested 3,000 others.

Civilian government was restored. Anti-military parties won control of the government in September of 1992. Prime Minister Chuan Leekpie headed a coalition of parties.

The Chuan government collapsed in 1995, due to a land reform scandal. Two new governments remained in place for very brief periods. Chuan Leepkie returned to the prime ministership in 1997. Thailand's sixteenth constitution since 1932 was adopted in 1998.

Years of government corruption and overvalued investments resulted in the collapse of Thailand's currency in July

1997. Thousands of Thais lost their jobs. Many lost a good deal of money. The International Monetary Fund provided a U.S.$17 billion aid package with stipulations that Thailand would have to begin new economic controls.

The suffering and confusion of the people were reflected in the results of the 2001 elections. Chuan Leekpai's government was defeated by a coalition led by Thaksin Shinawatra, a wealthy businessman. Thailand continues to experience steady economic recovery.

Togo

TOGOLESE REPUBLIC

Togo is located in western Africa, on the Bight of Benin. It is very narrow from east to west. The low-lying coast contains a series of inland lagoons. A plateau makes up most of the central area, while the north is more mountainous. The climate is tropical. The south has rainy seasons from April to July and from October to November. The north gets most of its rain between April and July.

The largest of the thirty-seven distinct ethnic group are the Ewe, Kabyé and Mina. About half of the people follow traditional animist religions. Thirty-five percent are Christian and the balance are Muslim. French is the official language, but numerous ethnic dialects are spoken as well.

The northern part of Togo was inhabited by Voltaic peoples for many centuries while Kwa lived in the South. The Ewe people joined the Kwa some time after the eleventh century A.D. The Ashanti, from Ghana, raided Togo to capture slaves for European traders in the seventeenth centuries.

Danish merchants settled on the coast in the late eighteenth century. Christian missionaries arrived and German traders displaced the Danes by the mid-1800s. The German protectorate of Togoland was established in 1884. Palm oil, rubber, cotton and cacao plantations were established. Railways and ports were constructed, and resources were developed.

Germany surrendered the area after it was invaded by British and French troops in August of 1914, at the outset of World War I. The League of Nations divided Togoland between Britain and France at the end of the war. British Togoland was incorporated into Ghana in 1956. French Togoland became a republic within the French Community in 1958. Togo became independent on April 27, 1960.

President Sylvanus Olympio banned opposition political parties in 1961, exiling his rivals. He was assassinated in 1963. Nicholas Grunitzky became president.

A 1967 coup d'état brought Lieutenant-Colonel Gnanssingbé Eyadéma to power. Economic reforms in the late 1970s were moderately successful. The 1979 constitution ended military rule, but confirmed the one-party state.

Eyadéma survived a 1986 coup attempt with the aid of French troops. Violent military action followed attempts to depose him in 1990. Eyadéma agreed to multiparty elections in 1993. He emerged the winner amid charges of fraud. Military violence and government corruption are a way of life in Togo.

GOVERNMENT
Website www.republicoftogo.com
Capital Lomé
Type of government Republic
Independence from France (UN Trust Territory) April 27, 1960
Voting Universal adult suffrage
Head of state President
Head of government Prime Minister
Constitution 1992
Legislature Unicameral National Assembly
Judiciary Supreme Court
Member of IMF, OAU, UN, UNESCO, WHO, WTO

LAND AND PEOPLE
Land area 21,925 sq mi (56,785 sq km)
Highest point Mont Agou 3,235 ft (986 m)
Coastline 35 mi (56 km)
Population 5,153,088
Major cities and populations Lomé 790,000
Ethnic groups Ewe, Mina, Kabye, numerous others
Religions Traditional animism 50%, Christianity 35%, Islam 15%,
Languages French (official), indigenous languages

ECONOMIC
Currency CFA franc
Industry mining, agricultural processing, cement, handicrafts, textiles, beverages
Agriculture coffee, cacao, cotton, yams, tapioca, corn, beans, rice, millet, sorghum, livestock
Natural resources phosphates, limestone, marble

Tonga

KINGDOM OF TONGA

An archipelago of more than 150 islands, Tonga lies north of New Zealand in the South Pacific Ocean. The islands form three main groups. The Tongatapu and Ha'apai groups contain low-lying coral islands. Tongatapu is the largest of the Tonga slands. About 67% of the population lives in the Tongatapu group. The Vava'u group is volcanic and mountainous. A volcano in 1995 created a new island among this group. The climate on the islands is tropical, with little temperature variation through the year. Tonga is often threatened by cyclones (hurricanes) in summer months.

The population is almost completely Polynesian. There is considerable outward migration to Australia, New Zealand and the United States. Tonga is almost completely Christian. Tongan and English are the official languages.

Tonga is a hereditary monarchy governed by a king and a legislative assembly. Only nine of the thirty members of the assembly are elected by the people. The rest are appointed by the king or queen.

It is believed the Tongan islands were settled in about the tenth century B.C. The first inhabitants were Polynesians from other Pacific islands. The Tongan royal family can trace its line back to 950 A.D.

Two Dutch navigators spotted the islands in 1616. The large islands were first seen by the Dutch navigator Abel Janszoon Tasman. British explorer Captain James Cook arrived in 1773. He called the archipelago the Friendly Islands. Methodist missionaries landed in 1822. Their success in converting the islanders was rapid. Virtually everyone on the island was converted to Christianity within thirty years.

Following several bitter civil wars, King George Tupou I came to the throne in 1845. He unified the islands and established a new constitution. King George Tupou II signed a protection agreement with Britain in 1900 to quell German colonial ambitions. Tonga remained autonomous, but Britain handled its defense and international affairs.

Tonga was ruled by the legendary Queen Salote from 1918 to 1965. She became world famous as the epitome of Pacific royalty. She was succeeded by King Taufa'ahau Topou IV, who presently rules. Tonga became fully independent on June 4, 1970.

A very severe cyclone caused widespread damage to the islands in 1982. A pro-democracy movement gained strength in the 1990s. Tonga joined the United Nations in 1999.

Trinidad and Tobago

REPUBLIC OF TRINIDAD AND TOBAGO

The islands of Trinidad and Tobago are northeast of Venezuela in the Caribbean Sea. Trinidad, the larger island, has three small mountain ranges. Coastal regions are low-lying with many swamps. The famous Pitch Lake in southwestern Trinidad yields large quantities of asphalt. Tobago is volcanic, with a mountainous central region. Both islands are heavily forested. The climate is tropical, with a rainy season from June to December.

Forty percent of the population is descended from African slaves. Forty percent are from East Indian indentured laborers. More than half the population is Christian, twenty-four percent is Hindu and six percent is Muslim. English is the official language, but Hindi, Spanish and a French patois are widely spoken.

The original Arawak inhabitants were joined by Caribs from South America. Christopher Columbus claimed both islands for Spain in 1498. The Spanish colonized Trinidad in 1532 and appointed a governor. Indigenous people died out very quickly from disease or abuse. Africans were brought in to work as slaves on the plantations. Trinidad fell to the British in the early nineteenth century. They abolished slavery. People were brought from Indian to work as indentured laborers.

Tobago was controlled by the Spanish, followed by the British, Dutch and French. It came under British control in 1814. Tobago formed a part of the Windward Islands Colony in 1889, when it was joined to Trinidad.

The islands were incorporated into the West Indies Federation in 1958. Trinidad and Tobago became an independent state on August 31, 1962. Eric Williams, leader of the People's National Movement (PNM), was prime minister.

The nation faced a serious economic crisis in the early 1970s. Rioting erupted, resulting in many deaths and injuries. A state of emergency was declared when a short-lived mutiny of the army was attempted. Intermittent violence continued into the 1980s.

A.N.R. Robinson launched a tough austerity program after his election to the prime ministership in 1986. Muslim extremists seized parliament and took Robinson hostage in July of 1990.

Continuation of the austerity program and privatization of state industries provoked considerable unrest across the islands. The trade-union dominated United National Congress (UNC), led by Basdeo Panjay, won power in 1995. Consistent disputes between the UNC and PNM have made the work of parliament very difficult.

GOVERNMENT
Website www.gov.tt
Capital Port-of-Spain
Type of government Republic
Independence from Britain
August 31, 1962
Voting Universal adult suffrage
Head of state President
Head of government Prime Minister
Constitution 1976
Legislature
Bicameral Parliament
House of Representatives (lower house), Senate (upper house)
Judiciary Supreme Court of Judicature
Member of Caricom, CN, IMF, OAS, UN, UNESCO, WHO, WTO

LAND AND PEOPLE
Land area 1,980 sq mi
(5,128 sq km)
Highest point
El Cerro del Aripo 3,085 ft (940 m)
Coastline 225 mi (362 km)
Population 1,169,682
Major cities and populations
Chaguanas 56,000
Port-of-Spain 53,000
Ethnic groups
African 40%,
Indian 40%, African-Indian 13%,
Religions Christianity 60%,
Hinduism 24%, Islam 6%
Languages
English (official), Hindi, Spanish, French

ECONOMIC
Currency Trinidad and Tobago dollar
Industry
petroleum, chemicals, tourism, food processing, cement, textiles
Agriculture
cacao, sugar cane, rice, citrus, coffee, vegetables, poultry
Natural resources
petroleum, natural gas, asphalt

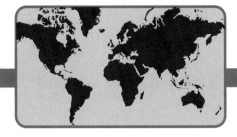

Tunisia

REPUBLIC OF TUNISIA

Tunisia is on the Mediterranean Sea in northern Africa. Mediterranean coastal plains give way to the Atlas Mountains. Arid plateau country south of the mountains gradually leads to the barren Sahara Desert. The desert occupies the southern 40% of the country. The northern areas have hot, dry summers and mild winters. Little rain falls in the south and temperature ranges are extreme.

Most of the people are Sunni Muslims of Arab or Berber descent. Arabic is the official language. French is widely spoken.

The original inhabitants were nomadic Berbers. Phoenicians founded the city of Carthage, near present-day Tunis, in the sixth century B.C. The empire soon dominated much of northern Africa and European coastal areas.

The Roman Empire defeated Carthage during the Punic Wars. It became part of the Roman province of Africa in 146 B.C. Vandals conquered the area in the fifth century A.D. It became part of the Byzantine Empire beginning in 534 A.D.

Seventh century Arab conquerors replaced the Roman-Christian culture with Islam. Egypt governed for many years. Berber Hafsites took over in 1230, giving the country its present name. The Hafsites were displaced by the Ottoman Empire in 1574. It established a semi-autonomous regime ruled by the Husaynid dynasty.

A Tunisian attack on Algeria resulted in a French invasion. The resulting 1883 Treaty of Mersa made Tunisia a French protectorate. Anti-French nationalist movements grew after World War I. Italian and German forces occupied Tunisia during World War II, until ejected by the Allies in 1943.

Violent demonstrations erupted after the arrest of nationalist leader Habib Bourguiba in 1952. Tunisia attained independence on March 20, 1956, with Bourguiba as president.

French refusal to vacate its naval base at Bizerte led to a confrontation which resulted in 1,300 Tunisian deaths in 1961. The Tunisian government later assumed ownership of French lands within its borders.

Bourguiba made attempts to established better relations with other Arab nations. Most of those attempts brought short-lived alliances. Political unrest culminated in Bourguiba's overthrow by General Zine El Abidine Ben Ali in 1987. Ben Ali freed political prisoners, eased restrictions on the press, legalized opposition parties and cracked down on Muslim fundamentalists. He was elected to a third term as president in 1999.

Turkey

REPUBLIC OF TURKEY

Asian Turkey, the main area of the country, consists of the Anatolian Peninsula, which was known as ancient Asia Minor. It is separated from European Turkey by the strait of Bosporus, the Sea of Marmara and the strait of Dardanelles. Much of the northwestern region of the Sea of Marmara is fertile farmland. The Pontic Mountains dominate the northern areas near the Black Sea. The central plateau lies south of those mountains. The early highlands region is the most mountainous and rugged area of Turkey. The major river system is that of the Tigris and Euphrates, which flow southeast into Syria and Iraq. Turkey is subject to frequent earthquakes.

The climate is Mediterranean. Summers on the coast are hot and dry, winters mild and wet. Winter temperatures drop well below freezing in the northeast. The west receives the most rain. Parts of the east are semi-arid.

About 74 percent of the population lives in urban areas. Eighty-five percent are Turks who descended from the Ottomans. The balance are Kurds, most of whom live in the southeast.

Most of Turkey's people are Sunni Muslims. There is a

Istanbul's Blue Mosque.

minority of Shi'ite Muslims in the southeast. There are very small numbers of Christians and Jews. Turkish is the official language. Kurdish is spoken by the Kurd minority.

Agriculture in Turkey was traditionally limited by primitive methods and a lack of water to many areas. The Tigris and Euphrates Rivers were dammed for irrigation and hydroelectricity in the 1990s. Developers are hoping to create a prosperous agricultural region in the southeast.

The key agricultural crops are wheat, barley, rye, olives, corn, figs, beet sugar, raisins and fruits. Manufacturing centers on processed foods, iron, steel, clothing and textiles, chemicals, cement, carpets and pottery. Iron ore, lignite, chromium, coal and copper are extensively mined. Turkey's highway and railroad systems are particularly well developed.

The members of the unicameral Grand National Assembly are elected by the people, under a proportional representation system, for five years. Assembly members elect a president who serves for seven years. The president appoints a prime minister from the ranks of assembly members.

Turkey, as it exists today, came into being after World War I. The region was dominated by sixteen tribal groups in 2000 B.C. Macedonia's Alexan-

der the Great conquered the Asia Minor region in the fourth century B.C. The empire crumbled after Alexander's death. The region fell to the Roman Empire.

Emperor Constantine established an eastern capital, called Constantinople (now Istanbul), at the entrance to the Black Sea, in the fourth century A.D. It was later conquered by the Byzantine Empire. Under Byzantine rule, Constantinople developed into the capital of Greek Orthodox Christianity. The Byzantines faced the constant threat of Muslim invasions.

The Seljuk Turks defeated Byzantium in 1071. They conquered the eastern part of an area known as Anatolia. The areas under their control became a sultanate in 1098. The Seljuk Turks, who had converted to Islam, repelled Christian crusaders from Europe during the twelfth century. Their rule fell to the Mongols under Genghis Khan in 1258.

The Ottoman Turks rose to prominence in northern Anatolia. They went on to conquer Thrace, Macedonia and Bulgaria. Their sultanate, established in 1396, was crushed by another Mongol invasion.

Sultan Murad II restored Ottoman power in 1421. His successor, Mohammed II, captured Constantinople and what remained of the Byzantine Empire. He spread Ottoman

GOVERNMENT
Website www.mfa.go.tr
Capital Ankara
Type of government Republic
Voting Universal adult suffrage
Head of state President
Head of government Prime Minister
Constitution 1901
Legislature
Unicameral Grand National Assembly
Judiciary Constitutional Court
Member of CE, IMF, NATO, OECD, UN, UNESCO, UNHCR, WHO, WTO

LAND AND PEOPLE
Land area 300,947 sq mi (779,452 sq km)
Highest point Mt. Ararat 16,946 ft (5,165 m)
Coastline 4,474 mi (7,200 km)
Population 66,493,970
Major cities and populations
Istanbul 9.4 million
Ankara 3.2 million
Izmir 2.4 million
Ethnic groups
Turks 80%, Kurds 20%
Religion Islam
Languages
Turkish (official), Kurdish, Arabic

ECONOMIC
Currency Turkish lira
Industry
textiles, food processing, motor vehicles, mining, steel, petroleum, timber, paper
Agriculture
grain, olives, beet sugar, citrus, livestock
Natural resources
antimony, coal, chromium, mercury, copper, borate, sulphur, iron ore

Turkey

FLAT EARTH PICTURE GALLERY

control to Greece, Serbia, Montenegro, Bosnia and Herzegovina.

The Ottomans expanded their domain south through Mesopotamia, Palestine and into Egypt. Sultan Suleiman the Magnificent conquered Baghdad, more of the Balkans and Hungary between 1520 and 1566. He failed in his attempt to capture Vienna.

The empire went into decline after Suleiman's death. European powers developed superior military strategies to inflict some disastrous defeats on the Ottomans. They were pushed out of Serbia and Hungary during the seventeenth century. Large areas of eastern Europe were ceded to the Austrian Habsburg Empire and other European powers under the 1699 Treaty of Karlowitz.

Russia began capturing parts of the Caucasus from 1720. France made a concerted effort to take Egypt around 1800. The Ottomans repelled them with British assistance. The Ottoman Empire continued its decline during the nineteenth century. More and more territories gained independence or fell to other major powers.

Conflict with Russia in 1853 provoked the Crimean War, in which France and Britain also participated. Conflicts between Muslims and Christians raged through the second half of the century. The 1878 Congress of Berlin resulted in more loss of territory for the Ottomans. The French took Tunisia. Britain occupied Egypt in the 1880s.

Radical reforms begun under Sultan Mahmud II gave the ruling class an increasing amount of power. Sultan Abdul Hamid II proceeded with major public works programs which revitalized the country.

Liberal reformers wanted controls on government power. They drew widespread support as they demanded a parliament to protect the rights of the people. Sultan Hamid agreed to a constitution. He accepted a representative parliament which convened in 1877. A subsequent war with Russia prompted the sultan to suspended the parliament and return to authoritarian rule.

A liberal opposition movement called the Young Turks demanded the restoration of the constitution and parliament. This began the Young Turk Revolution of 1908. The sultan and his government were deposed.

The Young Turks restored the constitution and parliament. Different political parties were formed. Muslim schools were secularized and women's rights were introduced.

The Turkish armed forces entered World War I as an ally of Germany. Invasions by Britain and Russia led to great devastation throughout Anatolia. Some six million people were killed in fighting or died from disease or starvation.

The Treaty of Sèvres in 1920 reduced Turkey to a small state comprising northern Anatolia and a region west of Istanbul. The Turkish Straits remained a demilitarized zone under international control. Led by Mustafa Kemal Attatürk, nationalists refused to accept the treaty. They set up a government at Ankara and signed a treaty with the Soviet Union.

Greece went to war with the nationalists in 1922, aided by other European powers. The Turkish troops, under Attatürk, were victorious. The resultant 1923 Treaty of Lausanne softened the earlier treaty's harsh terms. Turkey expanded to its current size. The Turkish Straits remained a demilitarized zone.

The Republic of Turkey was created on October 29, 1923. Mustafa Kemal Attatürk was president. The 1924 constitution removed the official status of the caliph, the Islamic spiritual leader, and created a secular state. The government and business structure was westernized and a European legal systems was introduced.

Turkey was officially a parliamentary democracy, but the Republican People's Party was the only active political entity. Sovereignty over the Turkish Straits was restored in 1936. Attatürk died in 1938. He was replaced by General Ismet Inonü. Turkey remained neutral through most of World War II. Its non-aggression pact with the Soviet Union was terminated in 1945. Turkey's allegiance moved to the West. It accepted Marshall Plan aid from the United States in 1947.

Adnan Menderes, of the Democratic Party, was elected prime minister in 1950. The economy began to grow under Menderes. However, his repressive government had begun causing serious dissent by the 1950s. Demonstrations by university students in April 1960 provoked a military coup. General Cemal Gürsel conducted a dramatic purge of the former government. Menderes and others were executed for violating the constitution.

A new constitution with a bicameral parliament was approved in a 1961 referendum. Turkey was ruled by a series of ever weaker governments. Leftsist movements spawned terrorist acts. The formation of right-wing terrorist bands to counteracts these events only increased the violence.

Shaky coalition governments and a deteriorating economy were the order of the day for the rest of the 1970s. The army staged a coup in September 1980. The National Security Council placed Turkey under martial law. It ruled for three years. Stability returned, but civil liberties were limited.

The Motherland Party formed a civilian government following a 1983 constitutional revision. Kurdish separatists in the southeast waged a guerrilla war against Turkish control of the region during this time. United States bases in Turkey were used extensively during the Gulf War in 1991.

A serious earthquake rocked northwestern Turkey in August of 1999. At least 17,200 people were killed, and 25,000 were injured. A second quake the following November killed an additional 700 people.

The 1990s brought continued tension between political secularlists and Islamic fundamentalists. Concerted efforts to curb inflation damaged the economy in 2000. A large loan was granted by the International Monetary Fund. Turkey continues to struggle with the rise of Islamic political parties. Turkey offered full-scale support for the United States' anti-terrorism campaign after the September 11, 2001, attacks on New York and Washington.

The Grand Bazaar in Istanbul.

Turkmenistan

REPUBLIC OF TURKMENISTAN

Located in central Asia, Turkmenistan consists mainly of plains which form the Kara-Kum Desert and its oases. The major rivers, the Amu Darya, Tejen and Murgab , are in the east. The Kara-Kum canal was built from the Amu Darya across the desert to irrigate arid lands and to supply water to Ashgabat. The climate is continental, with cold winters and hot summers.

Turkmens make up about three-quarters of the population. The other two substantial ethnic groups are Russians and Uzbeks. There are small groups of Kazakhs, Ukrainians, Armenians and Tatars. Most of the people are Muslim, following the Sunni strain modified by Sufi mystic influences. Turkmen is the official language.

The area of Turkmenistan was ruled in ancient times by the Persians. Macedonians under Alexander the Great replaced the Persians. Arabs invaded from the south in the seventh century. They brought the Islamic faith, which was quickly established in the region.

Turkmenistan was included in the Mongol empire of Genghis Khan's Mongols in the thirteenth century and Tamerlane in the fourteenth century. Uzbeks occupied Turkmenistan beginning in the late fourteenth century.

A Russian military base was established in the region during 1869. War ensued as the Turkmen resisted the Russian advances. Russia finally subdued the Turkmen in 1881. Sporadic unrest and uprisings occurred despite the repressive Russian administration.

The Red Army won control of Turkmenistan in 1920, after the Russian Revolution. It was included with Bukhara and Khorezm in the Turkistan Autonomous Soviet Socialist Republic the following year.

Turkmenistan became a constituent republic of the Union of Soviet Socialist Republics (USSR) in 1925. Guerrilla resistance to Soviet control continued into the 1930s. Islamic leaders were arrested and imprisoned in the 1940s under Russia's Joseph Stalin.

The independence movement regained its strength in the late 1980s. Turkmenistan made a declaration of sovereignty in 1990. Saparmurad Niyazov, of the Communist party, was elected president. Independence from the USSR came in October of 1991. Turkmenistand joined the Commonwealth of Independent States (CIS).

Niyazov had ruled with an iron hand, rigidly oppressing opposition groups. Reelected in 1992, he had his term in office extended through 2002. He was proclaimed president for life in late 1999.

GOVERNMENT
Capital Ashgabat
Type of government Republic
Independence from Soviet Union
October 27, 1991
Voting Universal adult suffrage
Head of state President
Head of government President
Constitution 1992
Legislature
Unicameral parliament (Majlis)
Judiciary Supreme Court
Member of
CIS, IMF, UN, UNESCO, WHO

LAND AND PEOPLE
Land area 4188,460 sq mi
(488,100 sq km)
Highest point Ayrybaba
10,299 ft (3,139 m)
Population 4,603,244
Major cities and populations
Ashgabat 605,000
Charjew 203,000
Dashhovuse 165,000
Ethnic groups
Turkmen 77%, Uzbek 9%, Russians
7%, Kazakh 2%, others 5%
Religions Islam 89%, Christianity
9%
Languages
Turkmen (official)

ECONOMIC
Currency Manat
Industry
petroleum products,
textiles, food processing
Agriculture
cotton, grain, livestock
Natural resources
petroleum,
natural gas, coal, sulphur, salt

Tuvalu

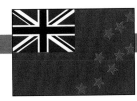

GOVERNMENT
Capital Funafuti
Type of government
Constitutional monarchy
Independence from Britain
October 1, 1978
Voting Universal adult suffrage
Head of state
British Crown,
represented by Governor-General
Head of government Prime
Minister
Constitution 1978
Legislature
Unicameral Parliament
Judiciary High Court
Member of
CN, UN, UNESCO, WHO

LAND AND PEOPLE
Land area 10 sq mi (26 sq km)
Highest point
unnamed location 16 ft (5 m)
Coastline 15 mi (24 km)
Population 10,991
Major cities and populations
Funafuti 4,000
Ethnic groups
Polynesian 96%, others 4%
Religions Christianity
Languages
Tuvaluan, English

ECONOMIC
Currency
Australian dollar
Industry
fisheries, tourism, copra
Agriculture
coconuts, livestock
Natural resources
seafood

Consisting of nine atolls, Tuvalu is located in the western South Pacific Ocean. The islands of Tuvalu are low-lying coral formations covered by coconut palms. No point is more than 16 feet (five meters) above sea level. The climate is tropical, with minimal variation in the warm to hot temperatures throughout the year.

The majority of the population is Polynesian. Almost all are Christian. The Protestant Church of Tuvalu is the principal denomination. There are small numbers of other Christians. Tuvaluan, a Polynesian–Samoan dialect, is the principal language. English is also widely spoken.

It is believed that the islands were settled in the fourteenth century by immigrants from Tonga and Samoa. British explorer Captain John Byron was the first European to visit the islands in 1764. It was not until 1826 that all the Tuvaluan islands were charted. They were named the Ellice Islands, after a British parliamentarian, in 1819. He had financed the expedition that discovered Funafuti atoll.

Christian missionaries began arriving in the early 1800s. The islands were a favorite place for forcibly recruiting indentured laborers for the Queensland sugar cane fields. Britain put an end to this practice by annexing the islands in 1892. They were joined with the Gilbert Islands as a protectorate. They became a crown colony in 1916.

The population of the islands peaked during World War II, when Allied forces occupied them. Ellice Islanders voted in 1974 for separation from the Gilbert Islands. The islands were renamed Tuvalu as a separate dependency in 1975. The country became independent on October 1, 1978 as part of the Commonwealth of Nations. Britain's monarch was head of state. Taorlipi Lauti continued as prime minister, a position he had held since 1977. The United States relinquished its claim to four atolls in southern Tuvalu in 1981.

Tuvalu has generated some U.S. $50 million in revenue from royalties paid by website addresses using its World Wide Web domain, .tv. The funds have been used to upgrade roads and airports. Electricity has been provided to some of the smaller islands.

The most critical problem facing Tuvalu is rising sea levels as a result of global warming. It is possible that some atolls could be submerged in the relatively near future.

Tuvalu became the 189th member of the United Nations in 2000. Saufatu Sopoanga was elected prime minister in 2002.

Uganda

REPUBLIC OF UGANDA

Uganda is on the equator in eastern Africa. The area of Uganda includes Lakes George and Kioga, parts of Lakes Victoria, Edward and Albert. The Nile River runs from Lake Victoria to the Sudan border. The landscape of Uganda is remarkably diverse. It features elevated plains, vast forests, low swamps, arid depressions and snow-capped mountain peaks. Uganda has a mild climate due to its altitude.

There are forty distinct ethnic groups, the largest being the Ganda, Nyoro, Soga, Toro and Nkole. There are tiny populations of Arabs, Indians and Europeans. Sixty-five percent of the people are Christian, fifteen percent are Muslim and twenty percent follow traditional animist beliefs. The majority of the people speak Bantu dialects. English and Swahili are also in use.

Various Bantu-speaking people migrated to the area of Uganda around 500 B.C. A fusion of these groups occurred. The first great kingdom, Bunyoro, was founded in the fifteenth century. Its armies brought much of central Uganda under its control during the next two centuries. The rulers of these areas were subject to the king of Bunyoro.

The ruler of Buganda declared his independence in the late eighteenth century. Two other kingdoms did the same thing. They all modeled their governments after Bunyoro. Arab traders from Sudan, seeking ivory and slaves, introduced Islam to much of the area in the 1840s. Buganda became very powerful, but it made no effort to subjugate the other areas.

British explorer John Speke, seeking the source of the Nile River, arrived in Buganda in 1862. Henry Stanley followed him thirteen years later. King Mutesa I permitted the entry of British missionaries in 1877. Rivalries developed between Protestants and Catholics in the 1880s. Factions developed and a civil war ensued. Frederick Lugard, of the British East Africa Company helped end the fighting. His successors used the Bugandan army to conquer the other kingdoms and tribes.

A British protectorate administration was established in 1896. The country was renamed Uganda. British settlers established cotton, coffee and sugar plantations at the beginning of the twentieth century. Migrants from India became prominent in the colony's economy.

The reduction of the king's power sparked a crisis in 1953. King Mutesa II was deported for two years because of conflict over constitutional changes. Ethnic and religion-based political parties were established during this time.

Crumbling colonial architecture in Kampala, Uganda's capital.

LONELY PLANET IMAGES – DENNIS JOHNSON

Independence came on October 9, 1962, with the monarch as head of state. Milton Obote was elected prime minister.

Obote's government was a shaky coalition of ethnically diverse parties. The constitution gave the various provinces considerable autonomy in efforts to minimize ethnic disputes. Obote suspended the constitution in 1966, declared himself president and abolished provincial kingdoms.

Major General Idi Amin staged a coup in January of 1971, while Obote was out of the country. He ruthlessly exploited ethnic differences, supporting the Ganda while purging other groups. He expelled 60,000 Ugandan citizens of Asian background in 1972. Many of these people were skilled business owners. Their departure and the general unrest severely weakened the country's economy.

Pro-Obote forces staged raids from Tanzania for several years. Amin's regime had killed 300,000 people by the late 1970s. He declared himself president for life in 1976. Ugandan forces invaded Tanzania, attempting to annex the Kagera region, two years later. Tanzania unified the anti-Amin forces and invaded Uganda in 1979. Amin fled the country.

Yusufu Lule became president of the devastated country. He was replaced shortly afterwards by Godfrey Binaisa. Milton Obote was swept back to the presidency in the 1980 elections.

A guerrilla campaign against former Amin supporters was launched by the National Resistance Army (NRA). Large numbers of Ugandans fled to neighboring countries. Obote was deposed by the military in 1985. The NRA invaded Kampala the following year, toppling the military government. NRA leader Yoweri Museveni became president.

Stability gradually returned as Museveni launched an austerity campaign and began privatizing state-owned industries. The tribal kings were reinstated, but without political powers. Ugandan troops supported rebel groups in the Congo during the 1990s.

Ugandans had become dissatisfied with corruption in Museveni's government. They were also concerned about involvement in the Congolese civil wars. Museveni was reelected in 2001 amid charges of intimidation of opposition supporters.

One of Uganda's greatest challenges is the AIDS epidemic. An estimated 1.8 million people had died of AIDS by the late 1990s. Another two million are HIV-positive. The country lacks the economic and medical resources to effectively fight the disease.

GOVERNMENT
Website www.government.go.ug
Capital Kampala
Type of government Republic
Independence from Britain
October 9, 1962
Voting Universal adult suffrage
Head of state President
Head of government Prime Minister
Constitution 1962
Legislature
Unicameral National Assembly
Judiciary High Court
Member of CN, IMF, OAU, UN, UNESCO, UNHCR, WHO, WTO

LAND AND PEOPLE
Land area 93,104 sq mi
(241,139 sq km)
Highest point Margherita
16,795 ft (5,119 m)
Coastline
16,006 mi (25,760 km)
Population 23,985,712
Major cities and populations
Kampala 780,000
Jinja 70,000
Mbale 56,000
Ethnic groups
Toro, Ganda, Nyoro, Soga, Nkole
Religions Christianity 65%, traditional animism 20%, Islam 15%
Languages
English (official), indigenous languages

ECONOMIC
Currency Ugandan shilling
Industry
sugar, brewing, cotton textiles, cement
Agriculture
coffee, tea, cotton, tapioca, potatoes, corn, millet, beef, dairy, poultry, cut flowers
Natural resources
copper, cobalt, limestone, salt

Ukraine

REPUBLIC OF UKRAINE

Located in eastern central Europe, the Ukraine has a coastline on the Black Sea in the south. Nearly two-thirds of the country is highly fertile steppes, which are lightly forested grasslands. The Carpathian Mountains rise in the far west and the Crimean Moutains rise in the south. The Dnepr and Dnestr rivers flow through the country and into the Black Sea. The climate is temperate, particularly along the Black Sea coast.

About 73% of the population is Ukrainian. Most of the others are Russian. Christianity, specifically the Ukrainian Orthodox Church, is predominant. There are small minorities of Jews and Muslims. Ukrainian is the official language.

Farming communities developed in the Dnepr and Dnestr river valleys during the Stone Age. Ukraine was inhabited by Scythians and Sarmatians after 1000 B.C. A succession of Goth, Hun and Avar invaders overran the area beginning in the first century A.D. The first community of Slavic tribes organized in the fourth century. They were instrumental in the establishment of Kiev.

Kiev became the center of the Kievan Rus. Since it was situated on major trading routes, Kiev grew and prospered in the eleventh and twelfth centuries.

The Ukrainian principality of Galicia was founded in the twelfth century. It was annexed by Poland in the fourteenth century. Kiev and another principality called Volhynia were conquered by Lithuania at about the same time. Poland seized Lithuania and its Ukrainian holdings in 1569.

Disputes with Russia over control of the region led to the Russo–Polish Wars in 1656 and 1667. The wars ended with the Ukraine being divided between the two powers. Much of the Ukraine was reunited as part of the Russian Empire when Poland was partitioned in 1793. Galicia came under the control of the Austrian Habsburg Empire.

Ukrainian nationalism flowered during the nineteenth century, despite Russia's attempts to suppress it. The Ukrainian Congress was established after the Russian Revolution in 1917. Ukraine declared itself independent on June 23.

The Ukrainians in Galicia began their own independence movement. East Galicia was put under a Polish protectorate

A street scene in the city of L'viv.

by the Paris Peace Conference in 1919. The government of Ukraine, led by Simon Petlyura, soon declared war on Poland.

Russian Communists established a Soviet government in Kharkov. They declared the Ukraine a Soviet Republic. The aggression of the Russian army caused Ukraine to become allied with Poland. They were too weak to defeat the Russians. The Ukraine became part of the Soviet Union (USSR) in 1922.

The Soviet Union worked to suppress Ukrainian nationalism until the beginning of World War II. Soviet dictator Joseph Stalin worked to crush the country's cultural identity during the 1930s. He appropriated most of the country's grain production for export. This led to a 1932–33 famine in which three million Ukrainians died.

Germany invaded Ukraine in 1941, during World War II. The people viewed this as their liberation from the Soviets. They soon realized that the Germans were solely interested in the country's natural resources. Anti-Nazi resistance movements struggled against them them until 1944. More than six million Ukrainians died when the country became a battlefield between Soviet and German armies. Over 1.5 million Ukrainian Jews were killed by the Nazis. Ukraine was ultimately retaken by the USSR.

The Soviets continued their work of replacing Ukrainian culture with that of Russia.

A nuclear accident occurred at Chernobyl, near the border with Belarus, in 1986. Thousands of people were killed and serious long-term environmental consequences resulted.

The Soviet Union began to crumble in the late 1980s. Ukraine declared itself a sovereign nation in July 1990. It separated from the Soviet Union as an independent state one year later. Membership in the Commonwealth of Independent States (CIS) followed. Former communist Leonid Kravchuk was the first president. He was replaced in 1994 by Leonid Kuchma.

The 1990s were marked by disputes with Russia over the Crimea region, nuclear disarmament and various economic issues. The vast nuclear arms stockpile left in Ukraine was transferred to Russia to be destroyed in 1996. Ukraine joined NATO's Partnership for Peace program. Russia agreed to pay for the continued use of the Crimean port of Sevastopol.

Little progress in developing a market economy has been made. Most major Ukrainian industries continue to be state-owned. They are generally outdated and inefficient. Kuchma was accused in the murder of a journalist shortly after his reelection in 1999.

GOVERNMENT
Website www.kmu.gov.ua
Capital Kiev
Type of government Republic
Separation from Soviet Union August 24, 1991
Voting Universal adult suffrage
Head of state President
Head of government Prime Minister
Constitution 1996
Legislature Unicameral Supreme Council
Judiciary Supreme Court
Member of CE, CIS, IMF, OECD, UN, UNESCO, WHO

LAND AND PEOPLE
Land area 233,100 sq mi (603,700 sq km)
Highest point Hora Hoverla 6,762 ft (2,061 m)
Coastline 1,729 mi (2,782 km)
Population 48,760,474
Major cities and populations Kiev 2.8 million Kharkov 1.6 million Dnepropetrovsk 1.2 million
Ethnic groups Ukrainian 73%, Russian 22%, others 5%
Religions Christianity 74%
Languages Ukrainian (official), Russian

ECONOMIC
Currency Hryvnya
Industry mining, electric power, ferrous and nonferrous metals, machinery, transport equipment, chemicals, food processing, sugar milling
Agriculture grain, beet sugar, vegetables, beef, dairy
Natural resources iron ore, coal, manganese, natural gas, oil, salt, sulphur, graphite, titanium, magnesium, kaolin, nickel, mercury, timber

United Arab Emirates

The United Arab Emirates is a federation of seven royal states, or emirates, located on the southern coast of the Persian Gulf. The coastline is marshy and low-lying. The rest of the landscape is barren desert plains with little vegetation. Temperatures are very high during summer. Dust storms regularly blow in from the northwest. There is almost no rainfall.

The great majority of the UAE's population lives in the cities of Abu Dhabi, Sharjah and Dubai. Twenty percent of the population are Emirates citizens, while the rest are guest workers. Fifty percent are Arabs, the balance are from southern Asian countries or Europe. Ninety-five percent of the population is Shi'ite Muslim. Christians and Hindus account for the remaining five percent. Arabic is the official language. Farsi, Hindu, Urdu and English are also spoken.

The emirates grew to prominence from the eighth century as trading centers. They were controlled by the Abbasid caliph based in Baghdad. The Emirates became favorite bases for pirates preying on shipping in the Persian Gulf. It was known as the Pirate Coast by the early nineteenth century.

Britain concluded a series of truces with the seven emirates in 1820. They officially became a British protectorate known as the Trucial States in 1892. The states became internally autonomous after World War II. Abu Dhabi's economy received a massive boost from the discovery of oil in 1958.

In 1968, Britain announced it would end all military operations east of the Suez Canal within three years. The emirates decided to form a federation. Abu Dhabi, Sharjah, Dubai, Ajman, Umm al-Qaiwain and Fujairah became the United Arab Emirates on December 1, 1971. Ras al-Khaimah joined the following year.

Oil price increases in 1973 greatly increased the UAE's wealth. Massive development took place and a substantial social welfare system was set up. There is ongoing friction between the wealthy and poorer emirates.

GOVERNMENT

Website www.uae.gov.ae
Capital Abu Dhabi
Type of government Federation
Independence from Britain
December 1, 1971
Voting none
Head of state President
Head of government Prime Minister
Constitution 1971
Legislature
Supreme Council of Rulers
Judiciary Union Supreme Court
Member of AL, IMF, OPEC, UN, UNESCO, WHO, WTO

LAND AND PEOPLE

Land area 32,300 sq mi
(83,600 sq km)
Highest point Jabal Yibir
5,010 ft (1,527 m)
Coastline 819 mi (1,318 km)
Population 2,407,460
Major cities and populations
Abu Dhabi 927,000
Dubai 430,000
Sharjah 280,000
Ethnic groups Arab 50%,
various Asian 45%, others 5%
Religions
Islam 95%, Christianity 4%,
Hinduism 1%
Languages Arabic (official)

ECONOMIC

Currency Dirham
Industry petroleum, fisheries, petrochemicals, construction materials, handicrafts, pearling
Agriculture
dates, vegetables, watermelons, poultry, eggs, dairy
Natural resources
petroleum, natural gas

FLAT EARTH PICTURE GALLERY

The spectacular Burj Al Arab Hotel at Dubai.